THE
OTHER SIDE
OF
CHAOS

Other Books by Margaret Silf

THE
OTHER SIDE
OF
CHAOS

━━━━━━━━━ † ━━━━━━━━━

BREAKING THROUGH
WHEN LIFE
IS BREAKING DOWN

MARGARET SILF

LOYOLAPRESS.
A JESUIT MINISTRY

Chicago

LOYOLA PRESS.
A JESUIT MINISTRY

3441 N. Ashland Avenue
Chicago, Illinois 60657
(800) 621-1008
www.loyolapress.com

Scripture quotations contained herein are from the *New Revised
Standard Version Bible: Catholic Edition*, copyright © 1993 and 1989
by the Division of Christian Education of the National Council of the
Churches of Christ in the U.S.A. Used by permission. All rights reserved.

Cover image © 2009 realeoni/Flickr/Getty Images

Library of Congress Cataloging-in-Publication Data
Silf, Margaret.
  The other side of chaos : breaking through when life is breaking down
/ Margaret Silf.
     p. cm.
  ISBN-13: 978-0-8294-3308-1
  ISBN-10: 0-8294-3308-2
1. Consolation. 2. Suffering--Religious aspects--Christianity. I. Title.
II. Title: Breaking through when life is breaking down.
  BV4905.3.S575 2011
  248.8'6--dc22

                                                          2011014937

Printed in the United States of America
17 18 19 20 21 22 23 24 Bang 10 9 8 7 6 5 4

For us the world happened

Between a mountain and a sea.

Somehow we were dislodged

Then we began to set ourselves free . . .

—RUSHDY SIERS, in *Words in the House of Sound,* 1999

Contents

1

Dislodged

The South African poet Rushdy Siers, author of the poem quoted in the epigraph to this book, knows about the chaotic world of change and transition. Born in 1952 in District Six, a neighborhood of central Cape Town, he grew up in the vibrant community of people for whom District Six was "home," a community comprising all kinds of folk who didn't quite fit the pattern that the then government of South Africa wanted to impose.

His neighbors might have been former slaves, immigrants, workers, and merchants. They would have been mainly "coloured"—South Africans who were neither black nor white, including many Muslims, and the Cape Malays, who had been brought there by the Dutch East India Company—as well as a few black Xhosa residents, some Indians, and a few white Afrikaners. Perhaps they had one thing in common: they didn't fit into the official boxes, and maybe that in itself was one of the reasons the community was so lively and close-knit.

When Siers was a teenager, the apartheid government suddenly decided to "clear" District Six. The residents were evicted and forcibly removed to a bleak area some fifteen miles away, called Cape Flats. Their homes were bulldozed, a living community demolished. And, as Siers expresses so succinctly in his poem, their world, which was lived out "between a mountain and a sea"—in the shadow of the mighty Table Mountain, and on the shore where the Atlantic and Indian oceans meet and sometimes collide—was destroyed.

The transition that he describes, with such ironic understatement, as "somehow we were dislodged," they would see in hindsight as the very point at which they began to set themselves free. And this freedom would eventually bring them back together in a new kind of community and transform the story itself into a lesson for all of us about the power of change.

As we make the journey through this book, we will explore what it is like for us, too, to go through upheaval, which often brings unwanted change in its wake and forces us through the narrow gateways of transition. I hope that most of our upheavals won't be as painful or as brutal as the one described in Siers's poem. Yet my own experiences of change encourage me to believe that it is often precisely those times when we are "dislodged" and forced to leave our accustomed comfort zones to embrace (or resist!) a new phase of our lives that we really do receive an invitation to "begin to set ourselves free."

What lies on the other side of chaos? Can an apparently negative experience of change be, for us, too, the catalyst for a new beginning, calling us forward into deeper freedom? No one knows, and none can predict. We will discover what new growth may be sprouting in our lives only if we risk the journey that takes us, like reluctant time travelers, hurtling through the uncharted universe of change.

Transitions are never comfortable.

They Make Your Feet Ache

You find yourself dragging crates and boxes around a new home, and what is supposed to be a familiar, cozy living space now looks like it would qualify for UN disaster relief.

You used to settle into your corner of the office in the morning, and now you are running a marathon before breakfast, trying to satisfy the unrelenting demands of a new baby.

You are trudging the unfamiliar streets of a town you hardly know, trying to locate a supermarket, a dentist, a post office. After the third time of circling the place, your feet won't tolerate a single further step—but where did you park the car?

They Make Your Head Ache

It's a great new house, but how do you get the telephone, broadband, even electricity and water installed? Where did you leave that long list of people to tell of your new address? How are you going to get your furniture up those stairs? How will you ever fit the contents of all those boxes onto so few shelves?

You thought you really wanted this new job. But now that you're here, do you really think you can handle it? You were so sure you loved this person. But now that you've made vows for life, you realize that life is a very long time indeed, and you may not even make it through to lunch without a falling-out.

You had your life together financially. Then you lost your job. What now? Where do you begin? Unpaid and unpayable bills? Anxieties about health care? Too old to start over? Too late to teach the old dog new tricks?

Worst of All, They Make Your Heart Ache

The last child has flown the nest, and you realize just how much you love her, miss her. You long for your son to come back to visit, yet fear that he might not.

You were someone in your job, a respected colleague. Now you are stuck at home with a screaming child, and you feel that you don't have a place in the "real world" any more. You are recently retired, and suddenly you have become invisible. No one asks your opinion any more. You feel unvalued, unwanted, unnecessary.

You wake up in the small hours and wonder whether, after all, you should have stayed in that crumbling relationship, hung on to your independence, remained childless and pursued your career instead, let the career go and had a child instead. Or you never even fall asleep, because your heart is churning and yearning for the partner who has died, for the home that the bankers repossessed, for the place where you knew the neighbors and spoke the same language.

Transitions Make You Ache Everywhere

They make you ache, in every joint and muscle and in every brain cell, and in every fiber of your heart.

Some of these transitions we freely choose. Some are thrust upon us against our will. Some just creep up quietly while we're not looking and take us unawares. But they all have this in common: they change us, whether we like it or not, and they usually don't give us the option of going back. Things will never be quite the same again, whatever course we choose going ahead. The flight path of time's arrow is irreversible. It moves only in one direction: forward.

So what does *forward* mean for us? Where are the meaning and the hope in all the disruption? Where are the petals of promise among the fallen leaves of our losses and regrets? Are times of transition simply chaotic periods that we have to survive as best we can, or might they mean more—much more—than that? Might they actually be times when something radically new is gestating within us and painfully coming to birth?

We all experience personal transitions as life unfolds. But today, the whole human family is also, collectively, living through times of unprecedented and accelerating change. We may feel as though all our old certainties are being stripped away. Our lives may feel dislocated and frighteningly insecure. We may find ourselves wondering,

"Where is God in all of this? Where is there any solid ground? How can we navigate these rapids?"

When my daughter was born, I had already been married and had worked in the corporate world for many years. But then I was—to my dismay—classified by the obstetricians as an "elderly primagravida." (Whatever happened to "Margaret"?) I turned, almost overnight, from a competent team leader in a responsible position at work into a helpless new arrival in the prenatal clinic. From being well informed about most aspects of my job, I was pitched into a situation where I knew nothing (I remember trawling the medical books to find out what "NAD" scribbled on my notes might signify and discovering, to my great relief, that it meant "nothing abnormal detected"). In fact, I was traveling at high speed in the fast lane, from confidence to bewilderment. I was out of control of my own life. My state of ignorance, and impotence, would only increase, I was to find out, after my child had actually been delivered, and with the additional weight of responsibility I didn't dare contemplate. No one can prepare you for the total life upheaval that a newborn brings, and the same can be said for most of our life transitions.

Why would I ever have chosen to put myself in the path of that kind of physical and emotional tsunami?

And I *did* choose it. She was a much-wanted child. Well, now, thirty years later, I could give you a thousand reasons why it was a good choice—probably the best choice I ever made. Her arrival brought new life not just for her but for everyone in the family, and for many more people whose lives she would touch. Ironically, she is an obstetrician herself now, delivering new explosions of change and growth into the world on a daily basis.

What if the other transitions in our lives were also births? What if all that pain and grief, that loss of control, that questioning and doubting, that fear and anxious anticipation, were also the labor pains through which something new and special might be breaking through?

Is there any meaning in all the madness?

In the pages that follow, I invite you to risk a journey into, and through, the crazy universe of change, both in your own life and in the life of the world. We will explore something of what change means for us and how we might live our transitions constructively and creatively. The journey will ask us to risk walking this shifting landscape of change and transition without trying to pin our life—or our faith—down into neat securities. It will challenge us to acknowledge that the state of change and flux is the reality that underpins all existence, and that if God is real, then God is right there in the flux.

We will take the journey lightly, knowing that the subject is far from light. We will do this because, as physicians have told us often enough, "It will hurt less if you try to relax"!

But we will also take the journey in faith—not the kind of faith that knows all the answers and has mapped out the right and proper paths, but the faith that says simply, "I don't know, but I *trust*." It doesn't matter what name you give to the power in whom you place your trust. It matters that you are willing to open your heart to a wider, fuller reality, one in which over time, or perhaps beyond time, you will know that ultimately every painful harrowing of your life's field, and every anxious tending of new and tender growth, are leading to a harvest that you can't begin to imagine.

2

Crisis: Danger or Opportunity?

I arrived back late at the nearest railway station one night
and took a taxi to my home. The driver was from Iraq and
had settled in England with his young family several years
earlier. He started to tell me about his experiences of life
in the West, many of them negative, and, rightly gaug-
ing my age to be a little more than his own, he asked me
whether life in England had always been the way he and
his family were experiencing it. My answer was immediate and definitive. "I grew up in a completely different
world," I told him. "I hardly recognize life here today as
the same planet, let alone the same country I grew up in."
What a difference a few decades make! And the past few
decades have made, surely, a quite unprecedented difference. Life seems to be moving faster than any of us can
react. There appears to be no chance of keeping up with

the rate of change, and our teenagers inhabit a youth culture that is completely alien to anything we ever knew ourselves. The only consolation is that in another few years, they will be the ones who can't handle the technology and will have to rely on their own three-year-olds to set up whatever device supersedes the DVD player.

My conversation with the taxi driver reminded me of some notes from a course I once attended on listening skills. The British Jesuit Gerard Hughes offered us the notes, which were titled "On Being Completely Baffled." We all laughed at the title, but the laughter was an expression of relief. Here was a proven master in the skill of spiritual accompaniment telling us frankly not only that was it normal to feel baffled in light of what we might hear but also that bafflement was "a good place to be." I have had plenty of cause to remember that wisdom as the years have moved on, and never more so than in the present situation in which the human family finds itself.

Surely the Chinese curse is upon us: "May you live in interesting times!" And the Chinese ideogram for *crisis* also comes to mind, with its combination of the symbols representing "danger" and "opportunity"—a combination we might see reflected all around us in our world today, to say nothing of in our own personal situations.

Everywhere we turn we see the immediacy of the danger. Across the street a house stands empty, repossessed by the bank because the people who called it home defaulted on their mortgage repayments. The elderly man who walks his dog in the park has lost his savings and worries how he will live on his diminished pension. The newlyweds down the road are caught in a spiraling debt trap, along with so many of their generation, seduced into living on expensive credit that seemed as easy as pushing a piece of plastic into a machine. Families in the flatlands are mopping up the debris after yet another unseasonal flood, in spite of their best personal efforts to stem the tide of global warming. And there are neighbors you just don't see anymore. Perhaps they have curled up in despair.

Danger! We see the possibility of catastrophic climate change; the threat of worldwide economic meltdown and the disappearance of all our financial securities; the constant and increasing danger of famine, flood, drought, and wide-scale starvation; the breakdown of trust in many of our institutions, including our religious institutions. Can humankind survive and deal with this level of breakdown?

The danger is obvious. But where is the "opportunity"? What if opportunity really is the flip side of danger in every crisis? Let's look at a few of the possible opportunities that may be concealed beneath these dangers:

- The opportunity to pool all our human intellectual resources to reverse the effects of global warming and rediscover ourselves as responsible living beings in a living planetary system
- The opportunity to embrace the fact that we are all interdependent and that the needs of any of us are the responsibility of all of us
- The opportunity to confront the greed and exploitation inherent in our current financial systems, to sit down together and work out a revisioning of how we conduct our economies
- The opportunity to face questions about what faith really means, how we will express it, and whether it really needs complex and corruptible organizations to make it work

If you are doubtful about whether there really is this connection between apparent breakdown and possible breakthrough, go back to the heart of the Christian story. There you will find a moment of total breakdown: the execution of Jesus of Nazareth. For his friends, this must have been a totally devastating day. They had staked their lives on this man and believed he would set in motion a whole new era of freedom. And now he had been executed as a common criminal, and they themselves were heavily implicated in the life and teaching of this "threat to national security." But this same ignominious death, this horrific breakdown, as we know, would become the gateway to an unimaginable break*through*.

That breakthrough is the paschal mystery of death transcended by resurrection. But are we willing to live true to the full implications of the faith in it that we profess and then let it play itself out? Are we willing to accept that things do break down in our personal lives and in the life of the world, and trust that this might really be the beginning of a breakthrough? Or will we try desperately to hold everything together, or put it back together, to how it was before it fell apart? In terms of our Christian story, we might ask whether we are willing to allow the death to happen, trusting in the resurrection. Or will we abort the paschal mystery by trying in vain to maintain the status quo, to hold on desperately to what is no longer leading to life, and thereby block the way to resurrection?

This is a question that will keep presenting itself as we move on in our journey through and beyond the chaos of change and transition. Are we hoping that God, or faith, will rescue us from the breakdown and repair the damage, or dare we trust that God is inviting us to engage in the coming to birth of something new, in and through the labor pains of loss and disintegration?

But let's enjoy a bit of light relief. Let's go back to the nursery and recall a rhyme we all once knew:

Humpty Dumpty sat on a wall.
Humpty Dumpty had a great fall.
All the king's horses and all the king's men
Couldn't put Humpty together again.

Humpty has been particularly accident-prone recently. He has fallen off the wall of climate stability. He has fallen off the wall of religious institutions. He has even fallen off Wall Street itself! And yes, it's true that neither the king's horses nor the king's men—nor indeed the world's financiers, politicians, lawyers, or clerics—have had much success in putting the pieces together again and restoring the system to its old state.

The truth is that once you have broken an egg, all you can do is make an omelet . . . unless the egg hasn't just broken but has *hatched*!

This is our story, in our lives, in our world, and in this book. It is the story of how something new may be hatching out of our own eggshells. The secret is to trust that this may be so and then engage with the task of helping birth the new out of the shards of the old.

As you look around you at the world we live in, and inside yourself at your own world, notice where you feel that there are crisis points.
In those situations, where do you see the danger?
Where might there be opportunity?
Do you think it is a curse to "live in interesting times," or can it be a blessing?
Have you experienced a Humpty Dumpty event? How do you feel about it? Did it lead—or is it leading—to nothing more than a rather messy omelet? Or is it a chick trying to hatch?

3

Mind the Gap

If you have ever traveled on the London Underground, you will have heard this warning: "Mind the gap!" It warns passengers that there is a gap between the step down from the train and the edge of the platform, in the hope that they will not fall down into it as they embark and disembark.

Gaps are usually considered hazards to be avoided. Children in times past played hopscotch—a street game that involved hopping from one paving stone to another in a certain order and not touching the gaps.

Gaps, it seems, are a bit taboo. They are bad news that might cause us to twist our ankle or be expelled from the game. A certain order, however, is to be greatly desired, whether in our behavior as we get on and off subway trains or in our adherence to the rules of the game, whatever the game may be, including the game of life.

Transitions are gaps.

They mark the gap between the no longer and the not yet. They are the space where we are neither in one place nor another, the hiatus between everything we thought we knew and all that lies ahead in the unknowable future. They mark the place where a certain order breaks down and chaos arises.

Some of the gaps between these spaces are well known to us:

- Having a house full of children and experiencing an empty nest
- Living prime-of-life action and living stay-at-home retirement
- Being self-sufficient and being dependent
- Being single and independent and being married or in partnership or community
- Feeling great and having to live with accident, illness, or physical diminishment
- Being married and being alone again because of bereavement or divorce
- Climbing the career ladder and focusing on the nursery
- Being a leader and being the new kid on the block

- Having financial security and struggling to make ends meet
- Leaving school and finding employment
- Pursuing dreams and experiencing disillusionment

Take a moment to reflect on whether you find yourself in any of these gaps. Don't try to fix anything, and don't make any judgments about yourself or others. Just notice where you are and how you are feeling.

Every kind of gap is a space between certainty and bewilderment. We thought we had it all together, and now we are not sure where to go or what to do next. We are on the edge of a strange new land, and we don't know its ways or its language. We are often alone on that edge and think we have no friends there, and that sense of isolation can be one of the most crippling aspects of transition.

Henri Nouwen, inspired by his encounter with the trapeze artists the Flying Rodleighs, captures this tension perfectly in the image of the trapeze artist, who has to let go of one bar and risk the flight through the air before coming within reach of the other bar. But the point of the exercise is really about how the trapezist handles the gap. What takes the crowd's breath away is the grace and confidence with which he flies through the air and that open question, every time: once he has let go of one bar, will he really reach the second bar safely?

A lesson to be learned from this image, to help us in our life transitions, is this: the space between the no longer and the not yet is an uncomfortable and risky space. We might not reach that second bar safely, especially since we feel as though we don't even know where it is and how stable it will prove to be.

But there is no shortcut to the not yet. We can arrive there only via the now. The "now" is the flight between the two bars. The now is where we really are, with all our doubts and fears. It is the only place in which we can experience and actualize the growth that is inherent in all transition and waiting for us to embrace it. It is our now that is shaping our future, whether personal or global. The now is the only place where we are really empowered to choose our path. It is like the pregnancy that both separates and connects the conception and the birth. If we try to take a shortcut around the gap, we will abort the new life that is asking to be birthed from within us.

There are two ways of avoiding the gap. We can refuse to cross it and cling rigidly to the no longer. That won't work for long, though, for the simple reason that the no longer is no longer there to cling to. The old job has gone. The old home has been vacated, and new people are living there. Our former health and strength have left us. The children have flown from the nest.

The other way is to try to reach the not yet too quickly, by leaping across the abyss rather than finding the right kind of bridge. We do this when, for example, we berate ourselves for not instantly being the perfect parent of the newborn, the recognized expert in the new job situation, the confident and independent single person when our hearts are still aching with loneliness. The fear of the gap can easily lead us into rebound reactions, such as when we take the wrong job too soon or enter prematurely into a new relationship after the breakdown of the old one.

Transition is the bridge that leads from the no longer to the not yet. Nobody can predict what that bridge is going to look like. It may be obvious and sturdy, and we may find it easily through the fogs of our bewilderment. Or it may be rickety and clearly unsafe, and we hardly dare entrust our weight to it. We will explore some of the shapes our bridges can take in the next chapter. The point is, however, that we have to cross the bridge, and as we risk that crossing, we will discover that the bridge itself is our guide and mentor, and it has everything to teach us about the path that lies ahead, beyond the transition. In fact, we will learn much more on that bridge, about ourselves, about life, and about God, in our transitions than on all the smoother pathways that we journey.

It turns out, in fact, that the gap is not to be avoided at all but is to be *minded*, in the best sense of the word. We are to pay attention to it, not because it is waiting to swallow us up into danger but because it is our personal, God-given tutor to prepare us for the next stage of our life.

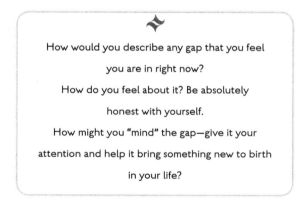

How would you describe any gap that you feel

you are in right now?

How do you feel about it? Be absolutely

honest with yourself.

How might you "mind" the gap—give it your

attention and help it bring something new to birth

in your life?

4

Bridges over Troubled Waters

A friend of mine once had what he called a big dream, by which he meant the kind of dream that lives on with you long after waking and shapes the way you see life in the future. Big dreams are often prophetic in some way, or they provide some kind of guidance, though often in a coded and cryptic form, by means of vivid images or a play on words.

This friend described his dream like this: "I was standing on the edge of a wide and fast-flowing river, and knew I had to cross it. To one side of me there was a huge and elaborate bridge—a kind of dream version of the Sydney Harbor bridge—but something deep down warned me not to cross via this bridge. So I started to swim. It was a great struggle. The water was cold and the currents were strong. I made it almost to the other side, and glanced sideways just before reaching the other shore. Then I saw that the big imposing bridge had collapsed. I swam the last few yards to safety and was immensely relieved that I had heeded the warning to avoid that particular bridge."

When we are facing transition, we may well find big and obvious bridges that seem to offer an easy and safe route across the troubled waters. One of these is the "bridge of money." If we have access to that bridge, then we can walk across the water and avoid what appears to be a lot of inconvenience. We can stay high and dry, and even look down on those who are struggling to swim the rapids beneath us. It may get us to the other side of the difficulty. Or it may collapse halfway. The bridge of money often turns out to be only half built. It will get us only so far without challenging our imagination or creativity. But then it might simply end and leave us suspended in midair with no other way to proceed.

Imagine, for example, an elderly woman who has always enjoyed the luxury of a big house and has never had to do much for herself. Following the death of her spouse, she can no longer afford to keep the house and decides to move into a smaller retirement apartment. The proceeds from the sale of the house will, she believes, set her up comfortably in a new apartment, and she makes her decision on this basis. And then the housing market collapses. She has signed a purchase agreement for her new apartment and then finds she can't sell her old home. The bridge of money that was going to lead her safely and swiftly across the river of change to the next stage of her life has collapsed, and she is down in the water, unable to swim, because she never thought she would need to learn to swim.

Jesus warns us to make certain that the bridge is fully built before we try to cross it. He tells (in Luke 14:28–33) the cautionary tale of the person planning to build a tower (or a dream home or an ambitious project—call it what you will) who failed to work out how much the enterprise was going to cost before he got going on it. We can see the results of such failure of foresight in our own towns and cities today, and even in our own failed projects. Jesus warns his friends about the cost of discipleship. If you really want to go the distance, into the unknown of change and transformation, you are going to have to learn to let go of what you are hanging on to in your present comfort zone.

Collectively, in the Western world, we tend to assume that if we throw enough dollars at a problem, it will go away. We are learning, painfully, especially in some of the world's most intractable war zones, that this is simply not true. The money goes away, like water trickling into sand, but the problem remains, and grows, like weeds in the rose garden.

A bridge that is very familiar to me is the bridge of obstacles. I'm sure you know it, too. You are going through a rough time—maybe changing jobs or relocating or trying to adjust to a new situation—and just when you need the universe to show a little mercy and give you a helping hand, one thing after another goes wrong. In my experience, these things tend to be relatively minor, but, like sand flies on the beach, they can give you a really hard time and distract your attention and energy from the matter at hand.

Let's drop in on a middle-aged man who has just lost his job. He is stunned that after many years of faithful service his employer has let him go. He now needs to apply all his energy to working through this frightening new situation. He needs to seek different employment. He needs to work out how to pay the bills. The future holds significant open questions: "What do I really want to do with the rest of my life? Where will I live? How will I feed my family?" But in practice, he spends a lot of his time trying to deal with a succession of other difficulties: a parking fine that he has unwittingly incurred, a problem at school with his teenage daughter, a reminder that his driver's license needs renewal, a broken window, a car that refuses to start. You might call it the one-thing-after-another syndrome, and we all get it from time to time. It makes you feel like you are running an obstacle course.

As I write, I am in the midst of a house move and trying to order some furniture online. Yesterday all was well. The furniture was to arrive in seven days. My payment had been received and accepted. But today the supplier advised me that the bank is failing to authorize the payment, even though I know the sum is well covered in my account. I am told to call the furniture company. The new landline hasn't been installed yet, so every call has to be made on my cell phone. The numbers for banks, furniture suppliers, and anyone you might need during such times are premium lines, charging exorbitant rates per minute. Even so, I have to make the call. The supplier advises me to call the bank. The relevant department of the bank isn't yet open. I am to call back in half an hour. Another premium call, during which I learn that the bank's computer system is in a snit and isn't expected to come back to life for an hour or so, but then, as I am charmingly advised, there is no guarantee that it will come back at all anytime soon. Meanwhile, my order will be canceled unless I can persuade the bank to authorize the payment. My day began with a pleasant walk along the beach of a new environment. Now it is bedeviled by the sand flies of these minor but extremely irritating complications. I am walking the bridge of obstacles. Does it sound familiar?

What do these two bridges teach us? Well, we learn that the bridge of money isn't reliable, and its lesson is that we should learn to swim. In other words, we may need to tackle the underlying issues that confront us in life rather than relying on money to rescue us. At a personal level, this may require us to learn how to fix household problems ourselves or to make or grow things for ourselves rather than turning immediately for outside help. At a global level, it may challenge us to look at the deeper causes of the conflicts at which we are throwing our dollars and search for new solutions to those chronic problems.

The bridge of obstacles is a real nuisance, but it, too, has something to teach us. When I am dealing with all those extra difficulties, I (sometimes) learn a little patience. I learn that creation is not simply waiting on standby to do my bidding. I learn that usually people are not creating problems deliberately to trip me up, but that they themselves are working at getting the computer going or the car started. I come face-to-face with my own impatience, my egocentricity, and my unreasonable expectations of others. These are not comfortable lessons, but they help me grow, and the bridge of obstacles is a good teacher if I will attend to its lessons. Beware, however! When you are struggling through those difficulties, you might easily be tempted to give up on the whole exercise of transition, to sit down where you are, and to get stuck there. This bridge teaches us tenacity to keep going when things get tough.

But before we leave the subject of bridges, let's pick up what appears to be a rather flimsy contraption: the bridge of rope. In conflict situations, the first targets of enemy action are the bridges. If you can destroy the bridges, you can disrupt communication and movement across enemy territory. The biggest, most elaborate bridges are the easiest targets. The safest kinds of bridges are those that soldiers carry with them as they go: a length of rope and the knowledge of how to use it.

When we are in transition, we are going to have to cross some difficult terrain. The safest kind of bridge is the bridge of rope that we carry with us. This is a bridge that we are capable of spanning for ourselves across the troubled waters, and then packing up and carrying it forward into the rest of our lives. A bridge of rope like this is made up of strong and durable strands of our own experience and of the collective experience of our human family. Any one strand may appear to be fragile, but together the strands make an unbreakable rope that will help us cross the abyss of change.

For example, Mary has been a stay-at-home mom for many years, but now that her children are grown, she wants to go back to work. She feels very apprehensive. She no longer has much confidence in herself and wonders whether she will be able to hold down a job in the ruthless corporate world. No one is going to construct an easy bridge for her. She will, mainly, have to make it for herself, but there are many strands of rope in her own experience that will make such a bridge a real possibility. For example, she has all the years of experience in managing family life. These years have taught her many things:

- Human-resources skills—She has dealt with personal crises of her partner, children, neighbors, and friends on a daily basis. She has developed excellent listening skills and imaginative and flexible ways of dealing with problems. She has learned psychology on the job, and she knows how to apply it. She is, in fact, a proven expert in problem management.

- ◄ Practical skills in fixing the everyday breakages of life—She has learned about getting the car to start, getting plumbers and electricians to appear when needed, and managing without them when they don't. She can cook meals from leftovers and cater for a sudden influx of hungry teenagers or her husband's sophisticated business contacts at the drop of a phone call. Above all, she can multitask!
- ◄ Financial-management skills—She can make two weeks' money last for three; budget for larger family purchases; handle the delicate balance between what children want and what it is appropriate for them to get; and work out how best to invest any savings funds, arrange a mortgage, and stay out of debt. She is in fact quite a financial whiz kid.

No need to go on. You get the drift. But does Mary? Does she realize that the strands she needs to make the rope bridge that will take her from domesticity to corporate life are already there in her own experience?

We can trust the bridge of rope. It will carry us across our transitions, and we have the means to construct it wherever and whenever we need it.

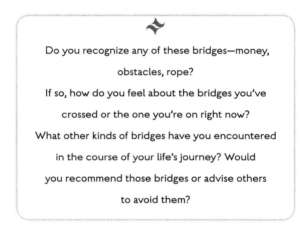

Do you recognize any of these bridges—money, obstacles, rope?

If so, how do you feel about the bridges you've crossed or the one you're on right now?

What other kinds of bridges have you encountered in the course of your life's journey? Would you recommend those bridges or advise others to avoid them?

5

When the Traveler Is Ready, the Bridge Appears

Crossing bridges is always, to some extent, a risky business.

In one of the Indiana Jones movies, the hero comes to the edge of a huge abyss. He must cross it in order to survive, but there is no bridge. A bridge, if indeed there is ever to be a bridge, will appear only once he has stepped out with one foot into the abyss. He has to make that first step in blind faith, trusting that the bridge will in fact materialize. If it doesn't, he will plunge to the bottom of the abyss. But if he stays on the edge and doesn't risk the gap, his enemies will overtake him. It's a bit of a no-win situation, but the magic ingredient is risk. Only by risking the unknown will a possible way forward reveal itself.

For example, Mary, whom we learned about in the previous chapter, will have to step out into her new job without initially knowing whether her rope bridge will help carry her across the gap. On her first day, she will be terrified that she might plunge to the bottom of the abyss, but then she will gradually see that she has more skills than she believed, and every step from then on will take her further across the abyss of fear.

If we as the whole human family are to evolve to a greater humanity, we will have to step out into the possibility of innovative, nonviolent solutions to global problems—solutions that rely on cooperation rather than confrontation and that focus on the common good, and not merely the advantage of our own group. Only then will we discover whether the bridge of our collective human experience will in fact carry us across the abyss of change that we are currently facing.

Are we willing to take those risks?

The question of risk is really the question of faith. The journey into the unknown future is a journey for people of faith—not necessarily people who have aligned themselves with a particular faith tradition, but people who are willing to trust in a power beyond themselves. Unfortunately, for many, the word *faith* has become

associated with certainty, not
not offer certainty. If we const
for ourselves, we can be sure tha
illusion. Experience will almost
apart, just when we most need it.

The story goes that there was
who made a living by pushing a
high wire that spanned an abyss. The crowds came out
in droves to watch him and to cheer him on. "Do you
believe I can do it?" he would ask them. "Oh, yes! We
believe you can do it," they chorused back in acclama-
tion. "So, who's going to get in the wheelbarrow?" he
asked. And silence fell. They all believed in him, but none
of them trusted him enough to get in the wheelbarrow.

People of faith believe in God. In the Christian tradition, the creeds set out fairly precisely what we are supposed to believe. We can recite those creeds as often as
we want, but that will not necessarily amount to trust.
In contrast, we can trust that, whatever shaky bridges we
have to cross, God, however we perceive God, is going to
be there with us, guiding us and helping us grow more
fully through our transitions into the people we have the
potential to become. We can risk the journey through

n, with God, without necessarily subscribing to statements of a formal creed.

An important bridge that we may have to negotiate before we go any further through transition is the bridge that spans the gap between, on the one hand,

> the assumption that faith means giving intellectual assent to a set of theological propositions, and thereby becoming associated with a specific faith tradition that is grounded on those particular propositions, having its own forms of religious observance

and, on the other hand,

> the realization that faith is really all about trust, and trust is something that only our hearts can offer, something deeper than anything our mind and intellect alone can achieve; trust is about surrender to the greater power that holds us all in being.

These two positions are not necessarily incompatible, but clearly they do not always come together in a neat package.

When we are in transition, belief is not going to be enough. Our belief has to transform itself into genuine trust. We are going to have to get in the wheelbarrow.

Take a moment to reflect on this question:

What does faith really mean to me?

One of the late Jesuit Anthony de Mello's images that is very helpful in our probing of what faith means, especially in the context of transition, when our former certainties about one or more aspects of our lives are in question, is that of the fish and the ocean.

De Mello describes a fish swimming in the water who has heard the rumor that something called the ocean exists. Desiring to know whether this rumor might be true, the fish stops other fish, as he swims, and asks them whether they, too, have heard the rumor about the ocean. "Oh, yes, we've heard about the ocean," they tell him. "So where is this ocean?" he asks. "Oh, we have no idea where it is," they reply. "Well, what does it look like, and where would I find it?" he persists. "No one has ever seen it," they respond, "so no one could ever tell you what it looks like or where to find it."

With this unsatisfactory reply ringing in his gills, what does the fish do now? Perhaps he decides that "ocean" is, after all, just a figment of the collective piscine imagination. Or perhaps he realizes that "ocean" is the entire mystery in which they all live and move and have their being.

I once told this story to a group of people making a retreat amid the rain forests of Malaysia. In the grounds of the retreat house was a beautiful pond, stocked with a population of rather splendid tropical fish. I invited the people to take time during the day to go and watch the fish and to reflect on the fact that the fish were swimming around the pond all day, looking for the water. When I followed my own instructions and went to watch the fish, I was intrigued to see that one maverick fish had decided to get out of the water and leap up onto a stone ledge. I watched it floundering around in its newfound freedom and independence until the need to survive forced it to flop back into the water again and resume its search for the source and sustainer of its being.

Those fish had absolutely no intellectual knowledge of the chemical constituents of water, or even of the physical existence of water. They didn't know where the water in their pond came from or where it flowed to after it trickled away down the mountain. But they trusted it to hold them in being, to provide them with all they needed to stay alive, and to give them the space and the possibility to be what they are.

Faith is about allowing ourselves to rest in the ocean of God's love and trusting that it will never fail to sustain us, whatever traumatic changes we may be facing.

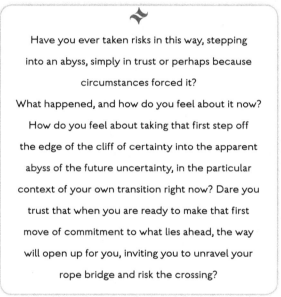

Have you ever taken risks in this way, stepping into an abyss, simply in trust or perhaps because circumstances forced it?
What happened, and how do you feel about it now?
How do you feel about taking that first step off the edge of the cliff of certainty into the apparent abyss of the future uncertainty, in the particular context of your own transition right now? Dare you trust that when you are ready to make that first move of commitment to what lies ahead, the way will open up for you, inviting you to unravel your rope bridge and risk the crossing?

6

God Bless This Mess

Transitions are messy.

Transitions are chaotic.

Transitions are where our hard-won order breaks down into disorder.

I remember well the morning when, after listening to all my outpourings regarding the chaos running riot in my life at that time, my long-suffering and very wise friend commented simply, "Just let the Spirit hover over the chaos." I stopped and thought about that image, a pretty amazing and truly foundational image in all faith traditions. This is how the Judeo-Christian tradition describes the beginning of our universe, expressing how some of our early ancestors imagined the dawn of space-time:

> The earth was a formless void and darkness covered
> the face of the deep,
> while a wind from God swept over the face of
> the waters   (GENESIS 1:2).

In our own times, Brian Swimme and Thomas Berry, in *The Universe Story*, have described it like this:

> All the energy that would ever exist in the entire
> course of time erupted as a single quantum—a sin-
> gular gift—existence. Space-time itself was tossing,
> churning, foaming out of the original reality, instant
> by instant. Each of the sextillion particles that foamed
> into existence had its root in this quantum vacuum,
> this originating reality.

Notice these common features in our human attempt to grasp at the remote beginnings of our story:

- Formlessness
- Emptiness and vacuum
- Darkness and depth
- Tossing
- Churning

And, surprisingly and unexpectedly, another common feature is the "singular gift."

These words describe the raw material of creation, whether you see it through the eyes of religion or of science. And then comes the transformative moment, at which creation as we know it begins. Look at the words used to capture something of this event:

- God's Spirit (also expressed as "a wind from God")
- Energy
- Sweeping (sometimes described as "hovering")
- Erupting
- Foaming forth

I read these accounts and then I look inside myself, especially when I am in the midst of flux and change, and what do I see?

- Formlessness: I can't get a handle on anything; nothing has its old shape anymore.
- Emptiness: I feel lost and lonely, with all my old reference points gone.
- Darkness: I'm in the fog of bewilderment, where there appear to be no signposts.

- Depth: Depth may well hold treasure, but right now it just feels really scary.
- Tossing and churning: I wonder what to do, how to get a hold on the new situation.

My friend recognized that morning that what I was sharing with him about my state of mind and heart was actually very much like the raw material of creation itself. If that were true, what might happen with this raw material if I could only let the Spirit hover? Might I indeed discover that what I perceive as a hopeless mess might truly be a singular gift? The action of God on the raw material of creation gives us a clue:

- A wind of change and transformation can blow across the dark void.
- A new energy can emerge, or even erupt.
- New possibilities can "foam forth," one by one, instant by instant.
- This is the singular gift of existence, forever renewing itself.

We don't need to understand quantum physics to recognize that these patterns of creation on the cosmic scale are also detectable in our individual lives at the micro-cosmic scale. What was true for the beginnings of our universe might also hold good for the beginnings of every new stage in any one life.

The message is really very simple: chaos is not bad news, a mess that we have to bring back into the right kind of order, the order that existed before we messed it up. On the contrary, chaos is a sacred reality, the very thing that is needed for a new creation to begin. Chaos is a gift, overflowing with potential.

Far from being bad news, theories about chaos have become a whole field of study in their own right. Chaos theory rests on the obvious fact that we recognize in daily life—that apparently ordered systems periodically fall apart and disintegrate into disorder. This is exactly what is happening in times of transition. The old system that we thought we had a grip on has suddenly gone to pieces. We tend to think that this has happened because we, or someone else, broke something, did something wrong, made an unwise choice, or disobeyed higher orders. In fact, during such periods of transition, we waste a lot of time trying to lay blame on something or someone in an effort to make sense of the breakdown of the old system.

Current thinking in physics tells us that actually our sense of being in breakdown is a reflection of the natural course of things and that breakdown is a necessary precursor of breakthrough.

There are specific features of chaos that might help us navigate transitions more creatively. First of all, chaos happens naturally and is not someone's fault. It is the flip side of any system. Without a period of breakdown and chaotic dislocation, nothing new can ever emerge.

Second, the process of chaos is very sensitive, and things can change rapidly and unpredictably in response to changing conditions. Small changes in initial conditions are magnified in a continuing feedback loop and take on larger-than-life proportions.

For example, my workplace might be planning changes that will involve some cutbacks and maybe even job losses. I get wind of this and begin to react negatively. My manager notices my negative reactions and gets the idea that because of my negativity I might be a suitable candidate for termination. I sense my manager's growing antagonism and become even more negative myself. This is a negative feedback loop, where each new twist makes matters much more critical.

On a global scale we could imagine a scenario a bit like this: One country somewhere in the world starts to flex its muscles and make belligerent gestures. At first these are only gestures because that country has no real firepower with which to threaten its neighbors. The neighbors, however, get the message and start to build up their armories "just in case." The first country picks this up and goes into full production to establish itself as a nuclear power. The world becomes agitated. Wild words are spoken. Eventually, even though the country in question still has no serious weaponry, others in the world decide on a preemptive strike "just in case." And the rest, as they say, is history. If it were merely history, that might not be so bad, but actually, this is an escalating situation in the world right now, and it is based on a negative feedback loop.

In his book *Chaos*, James Gleick sums up this tendency of little things to make big differences: "In science as in life, it is well known that a chain of events can have a point of crisis that could magnify small changes."

If you think of your own times of crisis, you will probably notice that during such periods of your life, the small things that go wrong can take on a life of their own and expand to fill your consciousness in ways that wouldn't happen in more stable times. These small things can affect your ongoing choices in a big way and even determine the outcome of the crisis.

All this turbulence will eventually settle down, drawn into a new steady state, but it will be something new—not just a return to how things were, but a leap, you could say a quantum leap, into how things shall become. Physics can prove it. Faith intuits it. We experience it.

And all this process of change and transformation hangs on the presence of that mysterious raw material: chaos.

We don't even need to ask God to bless this mess. If faith and science are to be trusted on this, we can assume that God is both present and active, in the formless void and in the wind of the Spirit. God is present, in the dark bewilderment and churning of our minds and hearts when we are in transition, and in the foaming forth of the new possibilities that—God knows!—lie latent within the mess.

✦

Take a moment to reflect on how your own inner

chaos feels to you right now.

Can you identify at all with the images from

either Genesis or from our new understanding

of physics and cosmology?

Can you trust that God is active, precisely

in the chaos?

Have you encountered situations that have begun

as small incidents but have taken on a life of their

own, escalating either negatively or positively into

significant movements that affect us all?

7

Can Bad News Be Good News?

There was once a farmer who had a son and a horse, and he was very proud and fond of them both. One day the horse got out and ran off to freedom in the hills.

"What bad luck," the neighbors commiserated.

"I'm not so sure it's bad luck," replied the farmer.

The next night the horse came back, leading twelve wild horses after him.

"What good luck!" cried the neighbors.

"I'm not so sure it's good luck," replied the farmer.

Soon afterward, the son went riding on one of the wild horses, fell off, and broke his leg.

"What bad luck," said the neighbors.

"I'm not so sure it's bad luck," replied the farmer.

A few days later, the army came recruiting, con- scripting every able-bodied young man and taking him off to war. The farmer's son was spared because of his broken leg.

Good luck? Bad luck? Does luck even come into it?

Bad things happen, and when we look back, we realize that good things sometimes come about not just in spite of but because of those bad things happening.

When we look back, for example, on times of personal upheaval that seemed so fraught with problems at the time, we can see that something new happened precisely because of those difficult times. Perhaps we grew in some way, or the universe changed the points on the railroad of our lives and took us some place we would never have discovered otherwise.

Pause for a moment and try to remember whether anything like this has ever happened for you. Can you remember bad times or unwelcome changes that seemed so unfavorable to you at the time, but, as you see in hindsight, actually brought great gifts into your life?

Depending on our upbringing and religious education, we each have varying images of God. We may think of God as someone who is waiting to catch us when we get things wrong or as someone who disciplines us and makes us go back to the beginning and start again when we mess up. I don't like or trust those images, because they don't resonate with my own experience, and over time, I am coming to see God rather differently.

Suppose God is continually striving to draw the more life-giving outcome from whatever we present? Suppose God, who is Life and Love itself, longs for nothing more than our coming to the fullness of who we can be, and will start over with us whatever happens, from exactly where we are, and lead us forward into the next stage of our growth? And, by the way, wouldn't this be what most parents want for their children, and isn't this the way most parents encourage their children—not by censuring them over and over, but by being with them where they are, whatever the mess, and helping them move forward from that point?

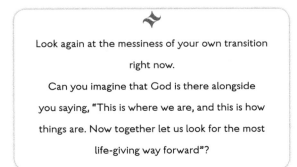

Look again at the messiness of your own transition right now.

Can you imagine that God is there alongside you saying, "This is where we are, and this is how things are. Now together let us look for the most life-giving way forward"?

The story of human life on this planet reflects this pattern.

Since life on the earth began, there have been five major extinctions, involving the wipeout of up to 90 percent of all life forms each time. These were, in the main, primitive life forms, and certainly the extinctions preceded the advent of human beings. The fifth extinction was of the dinosaurs. The sixth extinction, however, may be just around the corner, and that would be us!

The good news about these disastrous events, however, is that in every single case, two things happened as a result: a remnant survived the destruction, and that remnant continued to evolve, but its evolution took a quantum leap forward and became something radically new and more complex than what had preceded it.

For example, one of the extinctions happened because the oxygen concentrations in the atmosphere increased to dangerous levels, and most creatures simply burned up. Those who survived were the ones who learned to breathe that oxygen. Thus, what began as a disaster turned into a huge leap forward, leading to the beginning of respiration—a function essential to life as we now know it.

When the dinosaurs became extinct, rather suddenly, probably as a result of a meteor impact that caused a nuclear winter, the small-mammal life forms that had been hiding in the undergrowth came into their own. With the dinosaurs gone, it was the mammals' turn to take their place in the sun. The result, as every biology book will confirm, was a massive radiation outward of new forms of mammal life, including, eventually, ourselves. Bad luck? Good luck? It depends on how you see it.

Bad news can be good news. Bad news for dinosaurs was good news for mammals. But for Life itself, whatever happens will always ultimately become Good News, because life will prevail and flourish and change and evolve into more and more fullness of what it can be, whatever destiny throws at it.

If this is true for life as a whole, could it be true for us at the personal level? Let's apply this wisdom to our own transitions.

Always when disaster strikes, a remnant survives. The word *remnant* has a strong scriptural resonance. God often seems to choose a remnant of God's people to carry the divine dream forward in some new way. We will see this in action when we explore the story of Noah in the next chapter, for example.

What does the remnant mean for us personally?

I lived for a while in Eastern Europe, where sourdough bread was popular. I say this with due acknowledgment to the good folk of San Francisco, California, who have carried the tradition faithfully forward. People used to make their own sourdough bread by keeping back a little clump of the dough and using it as a starter for the next batch. A remnant of sourdough thus became the beginning of a whole new batch of bread.

When we are in transition, depending on how serious the breakdown is, we may feel as though almost every aspect of life has been disrupted. The old certainties, the old habits and comfort zones, have been dive-bombed. The old home, the old job, the old "me," may be almost gone. It may be the time to ask, "What is that essential core of who I am that remains through all this upheaval?" This is an important question, because it is this remnant that will be the starter for the new stage of our growth.

The thing about this remnant, this core of being, is that we often don't discover it until the force of change has stripped away the outer layers of past certainties and securities. Just as the seeds of the eucalyptus trees in Australia can't germinate until they are exposed to the intense heat of a forest fire, so, too, there may be deep parts of ourselves that are activated only when the shallower layers are stripped away.

And it isn't just about survival; it is about growth and transformation. The new you that comes through the blast of change will not be just a shadow of your former self, but truly a *new* you, with deeper layers of your personal potential exposed and invited to grow and flourish. For example, through apparent disaster you may discover skills you never knew you had. You may discover qualities that had never previously been called upon, such as resilience, patience, ingenuity, empathy with others going through similar upheavals, and even a sense of humor to laugh through the tears and glimpse the rainbow through the rain.

Can bad news ever be good news?

Yes it can!

Take a moment to sift through your experience

to see whether bad news has ever become

good news in your own life.

The skies are blue. The sun is shining. Noah is out in the fields inspecting his herd perhaps, or weighing when to start the harvest. He's a good man, and he has raised a fine family. He would make a sound presidential candidate!

Then he starts hearing voices. He thinks he hears God whispering in his ear, and what God says is utterly preposterous.

God says: "Noah, it's going to rain. You'd better build a boat."

Noah looks up to the heavens. "Come on," he says. "Look at the weather, Lord. Never had a better summer. What's this with a boat?"

God says, "Noah, build a boat."

Noah is getting edgy. "Have you thought what the neighbors will say if I start to build a boat, with the sun shining down so fine? What'll I tell them? They'll say I've lost my mind!"

God says, "Noah, build a boat."

Noah is a God-fearing man, and he isn't the guy to argue with God. So Noah builds a boat.

"Now," says God, "take a breeding pair of all the animals and get them in the boat."

(We will bypass, for our purposes, all the fine distinctions between the "clean" and the "unclean" animals, or the story will go on forever. And we will overlook the fraught question of whether woodpeckers and woodworms were included in the haul.)

So Noah does as he is told, still sweltering in the hot, dry weather, while the neighbors look on, shaking their heads and wondering whether to call a doctor.

The fine spell continues for quite a while, and everyone starts to pity poor, old, paranoid Noah. Then one day the heavens open, and it rains and it rains and it doesn't stop raining for months. The boat starts to float. The neighbors watch in disbelief as the flood waters carry Noah and family off into the sunset—except that the sunset is a distant memory now, as the sun is perpetually obscured by storm clouds.

Is this a picture of transition--being carried off by circumstances beyond your control into a world that seems full of threat and turbulence, and waving goodbye to everything you are having to leave behind, knowing that nothing will ever be the same again; traveling into the unknown with only a remnant of your former life on board?

Perhaps we are closer to Noah than we thought?

How life would have been on board the ark doesn't bear thinking about, but suffice it to say that eventually the rain abates. Noah tentatively sends out scouts to search for dry land. First he sends a raven, but the raven finds no dry land. Then, a while later, he sends a dove, but the dove comes back, having found nowhere to land. Another few days pass, and he sends the dove again. This time it comes back with an olive leaf it has found, so Noah knows that the floodwaters really are subsiding. At last, a few days later, Noah sends the dove off again, and this time it doesn't come back. It has found a place to land and, presumably, to start a new life in a new place.

And what is that new place?

For me, this is the main point of the story. The new place is on a mountaintop—the top of Mount Ararat. Does it matter where the ark comes to rest? I would suggest that it matters tremendously: The ark comes to rest at a higher place than it could possibly have reached had it not been carried there on the waters of apparent destruction.

When I reflect on all this, I find vivid images of my own transitions. I see how sometimes life has "flushed me out" when bad things have happened and I have had to start over with just what I was able to salvage from the disaster. Then I found myself, after crossing the rickety bridge of transition, in a place I could never have reached if the storm hadn't pitched me forth into this un-looked-for journey.

The story of the Flood has all the ingredients of a classic transition. Life is going more or less smoothly, and then circumstances change and the old order crumbles into chaotic disorder. Survival demands that we entrust ourselves to the chaos, with just a remnant of the old stability packed away in our back pockets, like a lump of sourdough with which we might be able to start another batch of bread, on the other side of chaos. Then, to our amazement, when the storm subsides and a new order begins to emerge, we find ourselves in a higher place than we could possibly have arrived at with our own steam. We have made some quantum leap forward, or the whole of creation has made a quantum leap forward, as we saw in the history of the extinctions that have marked the story of life on the earth. What we find there, on the high slopes of this new mountain, might be gifts we didn't know we had, strengths and skills that were lying latent and have been released only by the trauma of the transition, visions that we couldn't have seen from the lower ground we once inhabited.

The story of the Flood in the Book of Mormon, so I am told, includes a little detail that may also resonate with our own experiences of traumatic inundation. In this version of the story, Noah and his companions are bewailing the fact that once they batten down the hatches of the ark and set sail, they will have no light! This is a preoccupation that isn't recorded in the Judaic Scriptures, but it is clearly an issue. So what to do about it? The Mormon version of Noah turns to God for advice and is told to collect seven rocks and bring them into the ark along with all the animals. I can almost hear the protests of Noah's wife: "That's all we need now on top of all your menagerie— rocks, for goodness sake!" Noah doesn't have an answer either, but when the boat sails forth and the hatches are all sealed, imagine what happens: the rocks start to glow! They provide light in the darkness!

It's a neat extra touch to the story, but actually I think it is more than that. I think I may know those rocks. They are some of the hard times, the harsh experiences of my life, and when I reflect on them at a later stage, I realize that they hold a hidden power—they can become a source of enlightenment. I need them on my journey through transition, even though I may instinctively want to ditch them.

And above all of this story God spans a bridge. The rainbow, a phenomenon that never fails to stir our human hearts, arches across the skies above the stricken, struggling world, a silent, ever-recurring restatement of the eternal promise: Whatever chaos and breakdown occur in your life or in your world, though much may be destroyed, life itself will never fail!

★

You might like to read the story of Noah and the Flood again in light of the theme of transition. Does it speak to you in a new way? Do you find any resonances in it with your own situation or with the transitions we are going through as a human family in our world today?

Traditionally, it has been suggested that the story tells us that if we get in the right boat, with the right flag (the right denomination, the right country, or the right whatever else), we will be saved. I suggest that this is too narrow a view, that actually the story is reflecting the story of life itself. Breakdown can lead to a breakthrough we could never have imagined and bring us to a place of new beginning we never thought possible. It is, I suggest, not about the means to be "saved" and brought dry-shod to a safe haven on the other side of change. It is about the possibility of transformation and growth through the deconstruction of old and outgrown certainties. It is about trusting the waves of change to bring us to a new point of vision and future possibility.

We began by noticing that this is a story of how one man and his family—one "remnant"—came through a disaster situation to begin something entirely—or almost entirely—new. A characteristic of what happens when things become chaotic is that a new order emerges that, in scientific terms, is said to be self-similar to the old, which means that it has some characteristic patterns of the old order but contains the seeds of what is also radically new. We can assume that Noah, or the people who survived those ancient disasters, came through with a new, and perhaps cleansed, purged, and heightened sense of what it means to be human. We can hope that they moved on with greater insight than they had before, a little bit further from the law of the savanna and a little bit closer to the dream of God. We can hope! We cannot, perhaps, assume.

But in our own transitions, we can take hold of this dynamic more consciously. Transition gives us a chance to make a new start, to cherish the best of the past, yet risk the better of a future still unknown, to know that to make that future "better" is a task that lies in our own domain and depends on our own choices.

If we need encouragement to grasp at transformation rather than relying merely on rescue, we might take on board this wisdom that my daughter came home with recently: "Life is not about descending steadily into the grave with our bodies in a carefully preserved state, but about flopping in at the last minute, thoroughly exhausted, and exclaiming, 'Wow! What a ride!'"

9

The Rock and the Sand

"Stop the world; I want to get off" goes an old saying. Perhaps I would want to rephrase that and plead instead, "Stop the world, just for a few minutes, so that I can get my balance, please!"

When our lives crumble into chaos, we find ourselves forced to live one day at a time, or even one moment at a time, because everything beyond that is unpredictable, and the really hard thing is to find anything solid to stand on. We claim, as believers, that God is our "rock," but where is that rock when you need it? How do you find it? Will it really hold you? When everything is in turmoil, is there any safe place to stand and draw breath?

I have more than once expressed my distrust of clichés. Not that they aren't true, but they often allow us to bypass the real aching questions that beset us. The reality of God as our rock may be true enough, but when we can't feel it or see it, can we trust that it is really there?

How can we get our feet planted on it in the melee of our everyday reality?

One thing we may need to do is discover for ourselves the shortcomings of some of the things we thought were solid. I once watched some young children taking a swimming lesson. They were only just able to walk, and the teacher had rigged up a little inflatable raft in the pool. The idea was that the parent would swim with his or her child up to the platform and then encourage the toddler to climb up onto it and, holding the teacher's hand, try to walk across it, and then let themselves fall back into the water on the other side.

The children thought this was great fun. They probably saw the inflatable raft as a kind of island. Maybe, amid all this unpredictable water, they thought that if they could climb up on the island they would be on solid ground. But of course, as soon as they tried to walk across it, they discovered just how wobbly and how inherently unstable it was. I've no way of knowing how they felt when they flopped back into the water, but as I watched them I was thinking of Jesus' parable that goes something like this . . .

There were once two people who each had a dream of building a house by the seaside. The thought of hearing waves lapping at their doorstep and gulls crying overhead persuaded them to start building their dream houses. One of them couldn't get close enough to the seashore. He started to put down the foundations right there on the beach, in the sand. He built his house, and maybe he enjoyed the view through many happy sunrises and sunsets, but eventually the day came when the heavens opened, and the gales blew in, and the high tide swamped the sandy beach, and the dream house collapsed into a nightmare.

The other person, however, had thought about these possibilities, and, though it meant being a bit further away from the shoreline, had found a rocky plateau a little further inland and laid his foundations there. He, too, enjoyed his new home, and when the storms broke and the heavens shook their fists in the face of these human settlers, his house stood firm.

The moral of the story, as Jesus points out, is that if we are to survive, and indeed grow and learn through the storms that afflict us, we need to ground our lives on a solid foundation and not on the shifting sands of our own whims and fancies. The big question in all this, however, is what exactly is that solid foundation?

One thing I learned from the children in the pool is that the solid ground is not always what, or where, you think it is, and sometimes what seems inherently unsafe turns out to be the more solid option. The children thought the raft island was their solid ground, but actually they were much more unstable on the island than when they let themselves fall back into the water—they discovered that the water really would hold them in a way the island could not. The teacher was, of course, trying to teach them to trust the water, so that they would have confidence in its buoyancy as they were learning to swim.

What kinds of islands do we create, or try to inhabit, under the illusion that they are safe? And what do the waters mean for us?

Some of our islands are obvious. Frankly, most of us think that financial security is an island we can trust. We regard our health as something we can rely on. We look to our nearest and dearest to provide the emotional security we crave. We expect our food to be delivered to the supermarkets, and we trust that our technology will never let us down. We think that the earth will never stop providing for us and that things will always continue as they are now. We cocoon ourselves in these comfort zones, until the unexpected happens.

A catchphrase from the Monty Python era comes to mind: "Nobody expects the Spanish Inquisition!"

And nobody expects the call into the manager's office to inform us that we are being "let go." Nobody expects the stock market to crash or the bank to call in the loan. Nobody expects the accident or sudden illness that stops us in our tracks and dispatches us to the emergency room. Nobody expects food shortages, climate change, or the refusal of the computer to come to life in the morning. We never expect the unexpected, but every day we live, the unexpected is waiting for us around the corner. We have built our houses on the shifting sands of complacency and facile optimism. Then the storms come.

But sometimes the islands of security that we rely on are subtler. For example, we may well, and with truth, maintain that the Scriptures are a rock we can build a life on. Of course, sacred Scripture reveals deep truths that are absolutely foundational to a life of faith, but they become a rock we can stand on only if we allow them to penetrate our hearts and not just our heads. It is all too easy to "study" the Bible, and even to know it inside out, and not to have entered into its meanings and messages in ways that change our lives. It happens not infrequently that fervent Bible believers come up against turbulence in their lives and discover that their faith was only head deep.

This doesn't mean that Scripture is untrustworthy, but it means that maybe we haven't yet allowed it to penetrate the deeper levels of ourselves. One way we can help this happen is to practice scriptural prayer that invites us to enter with our hearts and imagination into a passage, to ask God for the grace to see what the passage is saying to us personally in our real-life situations. The question, then, is not so much "What are the facts here that I am being asked to believe? What actually happened, to whom, where, and when?" but rather "What does this incident or parable or passage mean to me today, and how does it connect to my own situation right now? What does it have to teach me about how to proceed in the most loving manner possible in this situation?" Such prayer fosters heart-knowledge. And it is in those things that we know in the depths of our hearts, rather than simply through the facts in our heads, where we will find a surer foundation for our lives.

When I ask myself, "Where is the rock?" I remember a time when an aunt of mine was bereaved. She had lost her much-loved husband and was in deep grief. She would not, perhaps, have called herself a person of conventional faith, but one day she asked me, "Margaret, where do you think he is?"

At first I was daunted by the question. The honest answer would have been, "I have no idea." An easy answer would have been the standard Christian response: "Of course he is with the Lord now, and at peace, and one day you will be reunited." But did I really believe that, and even if I did, could I have offered this answer to her without it sounding glib? I thought for a while and then decided to share something of my own experience with her. I told her about a time in my life—well, really it was more like a moment out of time—when all I can say is that I knew that life is held in a mysterious presence that we cannot name or describe and that this presence is utterly loving and all-welcoming. It felt like being immersed in that deep truth. It had been a moment that came out of the blue, and yet it has shaped every moment since. It hadn't been about "believing" anything then, but rather it was about a kind of knowing—the kind of knowing that afterward you can never not know. The kind that, no matter what anyone says, you know what you know, and that deep foundational knowledge is unshakeable. You can stand on it. It is a rock. Perhaps it is *the* authentic meeting place with God.

I told her, in a few words, about my own little glimpse of the reality of things—for it was indeed just a fleeting glimpse—and then assured her that this was all I needed personally to trust in that unseen reality for everything else, and to believe that my uncle's essential spirit was enfolded in that all-inclusive, all-loving reality. The assurance came from a conviction that was rooted in my lived experience of that reality, however momentary and fleeting, and I think it was because of this that it resonated deeply in her heart, and she was able to make her own connection with her rock.

For me, this moment was like discovering that, however shaky my own inflatable rafts may be when I try to stand up on them, the water itself—which looks so unreliable—turns out to be the medium that alone will hold me.

This doesn't stop my trying to make my own little islands of solidity, but now I don't put my trust in them the way I used to do. I still get upset and even panic-stricken when they let me down, but underneath all that, there is another kind of knowing that keeps on reminding me that the reality that holds me is infinitely more powerful than any of my false securities and is utterly trustworthy.

This same aunt of mine has a little sketch pinned up on her kitchen wall. It's a sketch of two ripe cherries that she painted herself at a time when my uncle had been critically ill but had recovered. During his illness she had been distraught, and while she was visiting him in the hospital in another town, a stranger in that town had befriended her and offered her a room to stay in during my uncle's illness. She had thankfully accepted this offer, and during her stay with this good soul, her hostess had tried to think of ways to encourage her to trust herself and her own deep resources. She had hit on the idea of inviting her guest to try to paint! At first my aunt had refused. She "knew" she couldn't paint, and she had other things on her mind. Then one afternoon, when she was sitting brooding about the gloomy future, something prompted her to try. To her own amazement, and to the delight of her insightful new friend, she painted those cherries. Now they hang there in her kitchen and remind her every day that when you think your own resources are completely depleted, something wholly new and unexpected reveals itself, and says, "Yes, you can."

Our conversation about where my uncle was returned to the topic of those painted cherries. My aunt had rediscovered the rock-solid foundation within her. She knew that her lost husband was in the place where those cherries grew, the place where the water holds you up and carries you forward, beyond yourself and your own limitations, when the illusory islands have let you down. Neither of us could prove it. We didn't need to. There are some things that you know, with a knowledge that comes not from the head but from the heart.

✦

What has happened in your life to bring you to an awareness of such heart-knowledge?

Where is your rock?

Next time you need to feel solid ground beneath your feet, go back to that memory—to that moment when you knew the reality of the unseen, and its loving embrace—to the insight or inspiration that revealed to you that you can do more than you think, that you have deep inner resources waiting to accompany you through this crisis.

10

A Fly on the Face of the *Mona Lisa*

Have you ever said about someone, or heard it said about you, "It's just a phase he is going through"? We say it a lot about children. When you are dealing with a small and fractious toddler, you know somewhere in your personal database that he is just going through the terrible twos. But when that same child is driving you demented with his tantrums, you can be forgiven for thinking that you have generated a little monster who will never be civilized. Every parent knows those feelings of desperation that your child will never be dry at night, will never learn to eat without spreading food all over herself and the house, will never speak coherently, and so on. With hindsight you laugh at yourself and wonder why you got so worked up about it, because you now know—and knew even then—that "it was just a phase she was going through."

An important aspect of living through change and transition is the ability to take the longer view. A fly walking across a work of art such as the *Mona Lisa* would have absolutely no chance of making sense of what was beneath its feet. Even we, who think we can see the whole picture are hard-pressed to express what this painting means to us! The *Mona Lisa* is mysterious. Life is the same. When we are stuck in one place, we can see only that tiny bit of the picture, and there appears to be no sense in it at all. We can't see the longer view—a view that may well be a lot longer than our own lifetime—so how can we trust it?

I live in a fairly isolated part of rural Scotland, with no street lighting, and indeed no street, just a country lane with passing places, surrounded by cows. But only a few months ago I lived in a lively market town in a housing development with lots of neighbors and bright—too bright—street lighting. So it came as a big surprise recently to wake up at one in the morning to find the house bathed in bright light. At first I thought I was back in my old home with the street lighting was blazing through my curtains. Then I remembered where I was and thought I must have overslept and that the dawn had cracked over me unawares. Then I went to the window and beheld the glory of a huge full moon, flooding the place with intense silver light. I was speechless under its spell.

Yet we don't get surprised and dismayed that it isn't a full moon every night. We don't get panicked when there is no moon visible in the sky. We know that sometimes we will see a full resplendent globe of moonlight, sometimes just a sliver, and sometimes nothing at all. That's the way it is. The moon goes through phases!

Perhaps the moon might consent to mentor us a little in dealing with our own phases of change. Taking the longer view begins by acknowledging honestly to ourselves where we actually are and then being willing to concede that this might not be the final word on anything, that in fact life is constantly moving on and that change will force us to move with it.

So may I invite you to take a little time here to reflect on what phase you're experiencing right now?

If you are like the new moon, then you are perhaps just beginning to see that something is shifting and changing in your life. Perhaps you have fallen in love and glimpse the beginnings of a new relationship. Perhaps you are looking for a new job. Perhaps you have relocated and are looking forward, maybe not without trepidation, to all that your new neighborhood will offer you and ask of you. Perhaps you are pregnant, with a new baby or with a new idea. Perhaps you are stirred by a possibility, recently revealed, to pour your energies into a cause for peace or justice. Perhaps you are wondering whether to take seriously a suggestion a friend has made that you should write a book. Perhaps an opportunity has just come up to further your education in some way. Perhaps you have a sense that you can no longer stay in the same fixed position you once held, regarding politics or religion, and you feel anxious about the implications of this shift in your attitudes. Just notice what you see.

With the full moon, life is flowing full and fast. You may be at the peak of your career, respected by many and carrying responsibility well on broad and experienced shoulders. You may be enjoying success in your chosen project or identity. Your book has been published. You have sold a piece of your own artwork or craftsmanship. You have basked in the reflected glory of your child's graduation from college and have settled back to reflect on a job well done in raising your family. You have built your dream house and now feel settled for life. You have cleared all your debts and enjoy financial security. You revel in your good health, your figure, your strong muscles, your acknowledged good looks and attractiveness. Your relationships are in good shape. Your neighbors and friends see you as a model citizen. Your light is shining bright and clear.

The last quarter is the moon's dying phase. We see less and less of it as the declining sliver of light shrinks night by night. There is much less light than there used to be. Things are not so well defined, so black and white, as they once were. You are no longer as confident and self-assured as you used to be. Perhaps you are facing retirement and wondering how your new lifestyle will feel when you no longer get up at seven in the morning and join the commuter traffic into the office, when you no longer hold responsibility for a large budget or a team of people. Or perhaps you are alone now, after bereavement, and you can't keep up maintenance on the family home. Your energies are declining, and you are thinking about residential care or assisted living. Perhaps the last child has flown from the nest, and you are wondering whether there is life after parenting. Perhaps you sense that your contribution to the workforce is no longer as appreciated as it once was; younger people are rising through the ranks, and you realize that you will never be CEO, or president, or pope. Perhaps the impending darkness unsettles you or even frightens you. Who will you be, or will you even exist, if no one apparently sees you any more?

When there is no moon, the light is out. Perhaps you are facing your own mortality. You wonder whether your life ever amounted to anything, whether the children will ever call or come back to visit, whether the cause you spent your life for has any future. Perhaps your religious order has no vocations, attendance at your church is flat, youth culture has taken over your neighborhood and you don't even speak the language anymore. Perhaps new technology has superseded the skills you learned as an apprentice fifty years ago and you feel redundant and out-dated. Perhaps even the values and attitudes you learned as a child—to be polite, to be frugal, to put others first and yourself at the back of the line—are apparently disregarded and even disparaged in what you see as today's world. Perhaps your friends have all died, and you are left alone, as the tide goes out on a deserted beach.

When we are in these situations, they can seem like the final word. When the light is rising and our energies are flowing, we think and live and act as if there were no tomorrow. Yet tomorrow will come, and where we used to run, we will need a stick even to walk steadily. Jesus warns Peter that one day someone will tie a belt around him and lead him where he would prefer not to go. And when the light is fading, we think the end is coming, and that's it. What was it all about? But if we can listen to the moon's wisdom, we will know that this no-moon phase is also the prelude to a new beginning, whether in this life or beyond or both.

Where do you feel you are right now? New moon, full moon, last quarter, or no moon at all? Take some time to notice where you are and how you feel about it.

Is there any sense in which you feel your current situation is the last word on things, that you are stuck forever in this place—whether it is a place of apparent success or apparent failure? Can you acknowledge to yourself, honestly, that this is just a phase you are going through? The dark phase will pass, as surely as the toddler's tantrums, but so also will the bright lights of success.

Jesus' own life was punctuated by times of huge success, when the crowds came clamoring to touch the hem of his garment, and also by times of apparent total and abject failure; times of brilliant light as he taught the crowds through his compelling stories and parables, and times of hostility and rejection, despair, and dejection. If we had only the story of Jesus' rousing successes, do you think we would still be following him today? Isn't it true that he was actually at his most powerful when he was hanging helpless and in agony on a cross?

One summer I planted two rosebushes in my little garden, in what was not worthy of the name *soil*, being mainly composed of builders' rubble. Nevertheless, to my astonishment, they flourished. Every time I came home from my frequent travels, I was thrilled and utterly surprised to find that they had brought forth even more buds. But because of my prolonged absences, I'm afraid they got almost zero attention from me. I hadn't done any of the things that the garden books say you should. I hadn't fertilized my rosebushes or clipped off the dead heads of the blooms because I'd been traveling. Those bushes were, I am ashamed to admit, left to their own devices. But whenever I returned, I greeted them and they greeted me back. They reminded me, ever so gently, that the dead heads, the wilting petals, the full blooms, and the vulnerable new buds are all part of their story—all at once, with no rhyme or reason in the arrangement.

On balance, I was quite glad that I hadn't interfered with them. Imagine if I had seen a dead head and got the notion that the entire bush was a lost cause, and then had ripped it out. I needed the presence of the fresh new buds to remind me that the whole rosebush was a bigger picture than the snapshot I was focusing on.

Life is always bigger than the situation we are in. Remembering that truth is a large part of what it takes to work through change and transition.

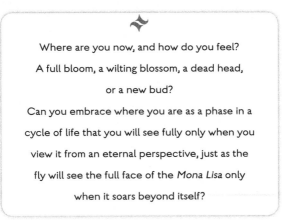

Where are you now, and how do you feel?
A full bloom, a wilting blossom, a dead head,
or a new bud?
Can you embrace where you are as a phase in a
cycle of life that you will see fully only when you
view it from an eternal perspective, just as the
fly will see the full face of the *Mona Lisa* only
when it soars beyond itself?

Perhaps the secret is to notice and respond to the passing phases but to live by the bigger picture, and to let that be our invitation to throw ourselves and our energies wholly into the moment we are living. We also must remember that the moment is a fragment of a much bigger story with possibly very different outcomes from anything we can imagine from where we are standing right now.

II

Strange Attraction

Sometimes it takes a bolt of lightning to release our creativity and kick-start the emergence of a new way of thinking or doing or being. Scientists say that it may have been like that when life first began to evolve on this planet, that violent charges from the electric storms raging above the crashing seas were the triggers for chemical change in the "primordial soup" where the elements of life were awaiting conception.

Certainly I have noticed this pattern in my own life. When times have been stable, and, though I might not have admitted it, there was plenty of time and opportunity to do something creative, I in fact became sluggish and stagnant, like a puddle of that primordial soup. Nothing flowed, and the days kept on coming and going with no movement forward. But when life fell apart and I had to adjust to new patterns, a new place, new people, and I was feeling stressed and pressured and didn't know how I was ever going to come to grips with things, then, for no obvious reason, I also seemed to become more creative. Ideas began to flow again, and somehow I found the time to explore and express them. The bolt of lightning had kick-started a new phase of inner growth.

In the bigger human story, history shows that it is often in times of crisis that humanity discovers itself. War, though it is an indictment of our failure to be decent and mature human beings, can also bring out the best in us, as we care for one another and work together in new ways to deal with the situations that war causes. Disaster often calls forth new depths of resourcefulness and altruism that we never knew we had. Evolution moved forward most rapidly when conditions on the earth were hostile, such as during the Ice Ages, when human beings had to invent new ways of surviving. We learn more from our failures than from our successes. Every failure is a potential learning point. It is said with some truth that we are often at our best when life deals us its worst.

It doesn't have to be anything as terrifying as a bolt of lightning. Sometimes just a small change in our situations can bring about a new growth spurt. Perhaps a change of scene, a journey, a visit with a friend, or even a book or a movie that excited new passion in us—all these can start a new pattern going in our minds and hearts and souls.

One of my favorite resurrection "stories" is the account of how a few of Jesus' friends, utterly devastated by his ignominious death, go back to what they know best: fishing. There follows a whole night of futile effort on the Sea of Galilee. They catch absolutely nothing. The experience must have emphasized for them the apparent futility of their situation. Everything they had staked their lives on had been destroyed, they thought, on Calvary. What was the point? Even the fish were refusing to bite.

And then the bolt of lightning penetrates the situation. Jesus himself is standing on the lakeshore, although they don't recognize him straight away. The dialogue that follows could so easily reflect something of our own situations.

"How's the fishing?" he calls out.

"Hopeless," they call back. "The water's empty! Not a chance! Might as well give up and go home."

"Try letting down the nets on the other side of the boat."

I leave the muttered comments from the fishermen at this point to your imagination. Even so, they do as he suggests and amaze themselves by hauling in a stupendous catch that almost sinks the boat.

"Now come ashore and let's have breakfast," the stranger invites them. "Let's start a new day with new possibilities."

The pattern here is a bit like that of the lightning strike kick-starting new life in the primeval waters of the earth, or of the unexpected and often unwanted change of circumstances that disturb our own stagnant waters into new movement and creativity. The unexpected appearance of a stranger on the shore, coupled with his unlikely advice to try fishing from the other side of the boat, to take a fresh approach to the problem, becomes the catalyst for a huge change in the way his friends will see things—and the way they act from then on. There will indeed be a lakeside breakfast, and it will mark the beginning of a whole new set of possibilities, based on the discovery that the man they had followed is leading them even more powerfully now than he did before his death.

This pattern is well known to science, too. Physicists speak of a mystery they call the strange attractor. It is a premise of chaos theory that, just as order periodically breaks down into chaos, within the chaos there is a new order trying to reveal itself. Just what form the new order will take seems to be determined, in ways that cannot be predicted, by this mysterious force, the strange attractor, at work in the heart of the chaos. We don't need to understand the science to recognize that something similar seems to happen in our lives from time to time, and perhaps in the life of the whole human family. As a Christian, for example, I choose to think of Jesus of Nazareth, and especially the energy released into the world after his resurrection, which we call the Holy Spirit, as a kind of "strange attractor," bringing about radical and unpredictable change in the chaos of the human journey as well as our personal journeys.

We will often find the evidence of this mystery at work in our lives and in our world precisely when our ordered systems break down into the chaos we wish so much to bring under control. My aunt, you may recall, in her distress, met this strange attractor when her hostess invited her to discover a new place within herself—"the other side of the boat"—and there she did find deeper inner resources that she didn't know she had. It was a very gentle lightning strike, but it stirred up a fresh attitude and a new beginning, a new order beginning to reveal itself at the heart of the chaos of her anxieties.

How can we learn to discern and to respond to the nudging of this strange attraction that is inviting us to move beyond where we are, to become what we can't yet imagine? There are three important things I would want to suggest.

First, we have to be willing to let things die, when the time is right.

Second, we have to be willing to tolerate, and even welcome, interruptions to the smooth running of our lives.

Third, we need to learn to listen to the subtle movements in our hearts that help us get in touch with whatever strange attraction is working within us. We need to listen to the movements of the Holy Spirit.

Letting Things Die

We possess a strong tendency to hang on to what we know, and we are reluctant to risk letting go of the familiar to make way for what we don't yet know. This is a bit like hanging on to the life of a terminally ill patient and refusing to switch off the life-support machine even when the patient has no chance of surviving We hold on, for example, to institutions that are clearly dying or dead and are beginning to turn toxic. We hold on to ways of doing things that may have worked when we were young but have been superseded by several new generations. For Christians, to refuse to let things die when their time has come is tantamount to saying that we don't believe in resurrection. Jesus reminds us that a seed has to fall into the ground and die, rot, and disintegrate before the new life can sprout from it. When we are in the crisis of transition, we are acutely aware of this dynamic working itself out in our own situations.

Permitting Interruptions

I hate being interrupted. I safeguard my space and time quite fiercely, and often I learn through experience that it is precisely the interruptions I try to avoid that bring new life, new directions, and new challenges. I resist them. It is then that I need to think of the interruptions that punctuate our human story and our sacred story— of those crises that led to near-life extinctions in the past, of the disasters that demanded our attention and required that we put aside whatever we were doing to attend to the immediate need. In our sacred story, we believe that the ordered life of a young girl in Nazareth was dramatically interrupted by the conception of Jesus, and we gasp at the chaos this turn of events caused, not just for her and her family, but for everyone who would come after. We might wonder how things would have turned out if she had resisted that interruption! Perhaps one day we, too, will be able to echo her consent—"Let it be with me according to your word" (Luke 1:38)—and say: Thank God for God's interruptions!

Listening to the Movements of the Strange Attractor

If the movements of the Holy Spirit are a bit like the action of the mysterious strange attractor deep in the heart of chaos, we need to attune our inner ears to listen to what they are saying to us. We need to pay attention to the ways in which a new order is being invited forth from our apparent breakdown. Some would call it "tending the holy." Listening asks of us only that we take some time, regularly if possible, to be in our own deep inner stillness, where we simply focus on and pay attention to those stirrings that seem to come from beyond ourselves as well as from within ourselves. This may take the form, for example, of sitting still with our situation, noticing what is happening, what is breaking down, what is being left behind, and how we feel about it. And then asking for the grace to begin to recognize the action of God in it all, trusting that this is drawing forth the new thing. It's a bit like a pregnancy. We can observe what is happening as a new life grows within us, but we can't second-guess what that new life will look like when it arrives or what course it will take thereafter. Our task is simply to nourish its unseen growth; to be loving toward it; and to wait until, when the time is ripe, it will reveal itself.

We can, and must, think about these issues and tend the movements of the holy, in the life of our world as well as in our personal lives. For God is no less active on the world stage than in the silence of our hearts.

Have you ever had bolts of lightning strike into your ordered life and interrupt all your carefully laid plans? In hindsight, did they ever become catalysts for far-reaching change?

Is there anything you are reluctant to "let die" in your life, even though you sense that its time is over?

Is there anything you can do to nurture the practice of inner stillness and the habit of listening for the movements of the Spirit in your life?

12

When Bad Seeds Yield Good Fruit

This isn't a nice story, but it has a surprising outcome.

It was late at night, one evening in August of 2007. Helen Newlove hadn't been feeling great and had gone to bed early. Her husband, Garry, and their three young daughters were still up and about in the house in Warrington, in northwestern England. It was a pleasant residential area, but the streets had been plagued for a long time by gangs of youths who indulged in heavy drinking and roamed the town committing mindless acts of vandalism as they went. The Newloves and their neighbors had reported this behavior to the local police many times, but the police had not, so far, been able to curb the excesses of the offenders.

Tonight it would be different. The gang lurched into the street and vandalized Helen's car, which was parked outside the house. Garry, a very peaceable citizen who had suffered such attacks for years, thought that the time had come to speak up. He followed the youths as they ran to the end of the street and then stopped them and remonstrated with them. The entire interaction was caught on closed-circuit television cameras. Garry remained calm and reasonable throughout. Not so the boys, who punched him to the ground and then repeatedly kicked his head in, leaving him dying on the sidewalk as his daughters came to the aid of their father and called the emergency services.

Garry lay in a coma for a short while, until he died in Helen's arms, surrounded by his very loving and close-knit family, when the life-support was switched off. It was a brutal murder of a fine man in the prime of his life, a killing that left his grieving widow and children in deep shock and near despair. However, the event galvanized the consciousness of the British public. It left us all wondering: How has this binge-drinking culture been able to take over so many of our teenagers and our towns? Why are so many people so intimidated by the threat of violence that they dare not confront this kind of antisocial behavior while it is still in its early stages?

Are young people's lives so empty that they have nothing better to do than roam the streets wreaking havoc?

Viktor Frankl, in his book *Man's Search for Meaning*, asserts that there is one freedom that can never be taken from us—the freedom to choose our attitude in any given situation. His wisdom is drawn from his own experience in a concentration camp, where he tested this freedom of choice to the limits. Helen Newlove was to discover this truth for herself.

In every situation, we have a choice about attitude, if not about action. In particular, we can choose the passivity of the victim mind-set, the "poor me" that feeds on sympathy but never really moves on, or we can choose an attitude of actively seeking ways to draw good out of evil. This is what Helen Newlove chose, and her choice has had widespread consequences.

Barely a year after Garry's murder, with a traumatic trial behind her and the girls, Helen launched a groundbreaking project called Newlove Warrington. Her intention was to inspire the people of Warrington to lead purposeful lives and become proud of their city. It was based on the assumption that the majority of young people are good kids and, with a bit of help, can find ways to enrich their own lives and make the local environment a happier and safer place for everyone. Newlove Warrington has, among other things,

- ◄ Established a community radio station, offering information and positive messages about health, education, and social care in the area.
- ◄ Produced education packages for use from primary school through university level, including specially targeted vulnerable groups, that explain choices and opportunities to young people. These packages are being incorporated into the national curriculum and offered nationwide.
- ◄ Become involved with the alcohol providers' industry to work on the need to bring binge drinking among British teenagers under control and to limit the accessibility of alcohol.

The list goes on, and these projects have received endorsement and support from the highest levels of government. A spokesperson for the project interviewed recently was asked why this particular campaign is so successful. This was the gist of his reply: "Mrs. Newlove speaks with an authority that comes from her own direct and agonizingly lived experience. This gives her an authenticity that is rare, and people listen to her. They know that she is speaking from the heart and this in turn stirs their own hearts into action."

This story could be straight from the Gospel. Let's draw some connections.

The tragedy begins when one ordinary man has the courage to confront what is wrong, in spite of the threat of retaliation. He is doing the right thing simply because it is the right thing to do. He is doing, in his world, what Jesus did in Jerusalem. He knows the risk but puts his family and his neighborhood before his own safety.

When someone lives true to his or her best instincts, as Garry did that August night, the power of darkness will fight back. In this case, that power was working through three drunken teenagers, and that darkness swept over Garry and destroyed him. The threat is real. The destruction is real, as real as it was for Jesus of Nazareth on the cross. When we live true to the values of the gospel in specific situations, we may also provoke the darkness, and that darkness may actually destroy everything we thought we were.

And the Resurrection? Jesus died, and as a direct result of that death, his Spirit flowed forth in unimaginable power, and it continues to flow through open minds and hearts today, bringing transformation to the earth's situations if we will allow it and work with it. After Garry's death, a wholly unexpected spirit was released in his widow and is now flowing out into their community and into the wider world, bringing new hope and new possibilities of how a stricken community might become the seed of something new.

And finally, the mark of authenticity is personal experience. It was said of Jesus that his teaching was something else, something most people hadn't heard before—not because of its content, but because it came straight from the heart—a heart that lived in constant harmony and alignment with the source of all being.

Some of us may take exception to this apparent comparison of the life, death, and resurrection of Jesus with a story from ordinary life in Warrington. Yet I believe this is what God calls each one of us to do: to live out the pattern of Jesus' life and death in our own living. And when we see glimpses of this pattern in the lives (and deaths) of our neighbors, we are invited to learn from what we see.

Humpty Dumpty crashes, and the crash seems utterly beyond repair. It depends on us, and on our attitude, whether there is a new chick among the broken eggshells.

The moral of the story is that when we live true, we may face seriously destructive consequences, but that apparent destruction is not the final word. The Spirit of God, and the spirit of all that is best in humanity, can and does prevail to bring forth new life.

Have you come across any such stories where a positive attitude became the catalyst for transformative change in an otherwise destructive situation?
Take a look at any difficult situations in your own life right now. How would you describe your own attitude toward them? Is there anything you would want to change in your attitude?
As you reflect on the world's situations at this time, where do you think our human attitudes are encouraging life-giving change, and where do you see negative attitudes holding back such change?
How might we change our attitudes?
Stories like this reflect the dynamic of the gospel itself. Where do you see the story of Calvary being enacted in the world around you? Do you believe in the possibility of resurrection in such situations? How might you help that potential become a reality?

13

Places of Passage, Places of Fear

There was a time, not so very long ago, when most people still believed that the world was flat, and that if you sailed too far into the unknown, you would fall off the edge. Maps from those times would sometimes show images of dragons on the margins, as a dire warning for any who might be thinking of venturing too far—beyond the edge. Now, five centuries or so later, we know that every new horizon beckons to new discoveries and new growth. But do we allow this intuition to touch our journeys of faith? Can we honestly say, in our spiritual journeying, that we are no longer afraid that if we go too far beyond the margins of orthodoxy, we won't fall foul of the dragons or topple off the edge? Dare we really follow the dream that will always call us beyond the comfort zone? Or will our fears win the day and hold us back from the brink?

Our times of transition can be very frightening, as well as potentially exciting and challenging. Places of passage can be the images of nightmare as well as of dream. Facing our fears is probably the hardest part of journeying through transition, so it might be helpful to pause for a while to look a few of those scary places in the eyes. See whether any of these places of passage speak to where you find yourself. Use the images that appeal to you to help you identify what kinds of fears are besetting you and maybe undermining your journey.

Tunnels

Sometimes the only way to get through an apparently solid obstruction is to dig a tunnel. Venturing through a tunnel is not a nice experience, unless you are a caving enthusiast. Most of us feel uncomfortable in a tunnel, and some transitions involve going through dark, subterranean space. Perhaps you fear the dark of not knowing where you are or where you are going. Perhaps you feel you are being railroaded down a narrow constriction with little chance of choosing an alternative route. Perhaps you even feel that circumstances are suffocating you and that you long to breathe the fresh air of free choice again.

Mountain Passes

Pioneers may have to negotiate mountain ranges that stand between them and their desired goal. Crossing a mountain range exposes you to the elements and to the sometimes not-uncritical gaze of others. For myself, an off-the-scale introvert, I can say that being pitched into the world of public speaking has been, and still is, like crossing a very craggy mountain pass, where bears and mountain lions might emerge from the rocks at any moment and where strong mountain winds threaten to blow away all my fragile defenses. If your place of passage feels like a mountain pass, you may know how it feels to be terrified of falling, or failing, in the challenge set before you.

Causeways

A causeway is a place where a way opens up where previously there could be no way, for example, a path or road to a tidal island that is passable only at low tide, or a strip of terrain that is normally a swamp but becomes passable when it freezes hard in winter. The thing about crossing a causeway is the awareness that there is no way back. The tide is coming in behind you, and you must move forward. Perhaps your place of passage is a bit like that, and your dread of leaving behind all possibility of return is daunting.

Flight

Fear of flying is not uncommon, and sometimes our places of passage can seem to demand that we commit ourselves to very flimsy and very human constructions. Perhaps we dread being out of control in the situation or knowing that there is nothing we can do to ensure that events proceed as they should. It is a frightening experience to find yourself in a space where you have no choice but to trust another person—let alone trust God!

Rough Sea Crossings

The image of being at sea in a storm, with the waves crashing around you and the boat taking on water faster than you can bail it out, is a powerful representation of transitional places. Perhaps the fear being evoked here is the fear of conflict and turmoil. Perhaps you feel you have to fight to survive in this situation. Perhaps you are a person who dreads confrontation, and yet here you are, confronted by towering challenges on every side and tossed around by the conflicting voices of those around you—when what you really want is to please everyone.

Perhaps transition is taking you to a place where you are invited to be yourself, and to be discerning about how much you bend yourself into false positions to please others. Perhaps you are terrified of the risks you are taking, and you feel exposed to forces you can neither understand nor manipulate.

Cliff Tops

A stroll along the top of a cliff on a pleasant summer day is one thing, but to discover that your life's path has brought you up against the edge of a precipice is something else entirely. Perhaps your fears can be expressed in the terror of moving forward, lest you plummet down to the depths. Perhaps you feel dangerously exposed and afraid to take a false step in case it starts a landslide. Perhaps you are experiencing a very natural fear of falling into despair or that depression is stalking.

Jungle Trails

The jungle is brimming with all kinds of hazards, as well as all kinds of wonders. It is fertile space in which there is often luxuriant growth, but it is also full of wild beasts that you can't see—yet you know they can see you. Perhaps your place of passage feels a bit like this. Perhaps you know you want to keep on blazing the trail through all this wild fecundity, but you have no way of knowing where the hidden dangers lurk. Perhaps, in your situation, there is the proverbial "elephant in the room" that nobody dares to mention and name, in case everyone else gets upset. This is very much the case now, for example, in the places of passage we are navigating in our religious institutions. Nobody wants to be the first to mention that the emperor has no clothes on. Nobody dares to be the first to declare bankruptcy. The challenge in such situations might be, precisely, to risk calling things by their name and looking them in the eye. You might discover that more people know about the elephant than you think.

Desert Crossings

The desert is empty, trackless, and lonely. Perhaps your place of passage feels a bit like this? Perhaps you are feeling abandoned on your onward journey, a journey which may have alienated your former friends or even your family, who don't, or won't understand where your dream is leading you. Perhaps you fear the loss of status or popularity that your struggle through this transition may cause. Perhaps you are feeling rejected by those who once supported you but are now unwilling to walk the remaining miles of a journey you began together. Perhaps, as the desert winds whistle through your bones and the hot sand grazes your skin, you feel isolated, lost and very, very lonely.

None of these places is a comfortable place to be, because transition is never comfortable. When I was a little girl and complained of sundry aches and pains, a wise elderly aunt of mine used to tell me they were just growing pains. She was probably right. Growth is always painful in some way, and transition is always an invitation to grow.

The Celts, however, had an intuition about places of passage, and their intuition might be helpful to us. In Celtic spirituality, crossing places were considered especially sacred spaces. And so they honored such places as bridges, gateways, and causeways as "thin" places, where the boundary between the visible and the invisible worlds was more open than usual. These are places, or situations, in which God was so close as to be almost palpable, and the Celts understood sacred spaces like these as places of transformation. Where the invisible world interpenetrates our visible world, they believed, something new could come into being. You could say that sacred spaces were a bit like those mysterious strange attractors that act as catalysts for the emergence of new patterns of being and becoming. It's not surprising that, to Celtic Christians, Jesus was the ultimate sacred space, where the mystery of God interpenetrated and became incarnate in a human life.

Can we look at our own places of passage in this light? Dare we trust that, in spite of all the pain and anxiety and fear they may evoke in us, they are actually the thin places where transformation is very close at hand? That is, if we can trust the process and work with God to bring about the new.

I was in County Donegal in Ireland one summer, facilitating a retreat in a lovely little house beside a long and almost deserted beach that skirted a sea loch. We had been looking at the problems of letting things go, and I suggested to those on retreat that if there was something they wanted to let go of—perhaps some fear or anxiety or resentment—they might like to go down to the shore at low tide and draw some symbol of their preoccupation in the sand, and then the next morning go back to the beach and notice how, while they had slept, the advancing and receding tides had washed away their symbol. It felt only right to do this exercise myself, and so that evening I made a sign in the sand that represented a situation I was anxious about. As I made my symbol, I realized that it was helping me clarify exactly what it was I was so angry about and so afraid of. Drawing in the sand had, that night, the same effect as speaking out my concerns to a wise friend. It was also a way of turning my anxieties into prayer.

The next day I returned home. It happened that the anxiety I had been contemplating came up in conversation—no coincidence I'm sure! I learned that the person around whom these anxieties centered was going away the day after the following. Something inside me said, "Hey, Margaret, pictures in the sand are all well and good, and yes, the tide will wash them away, but this thing becomes real and effective only if you do something about it. You have precisely twenty-four hours to do something about it. What are you going to do?"

I did do something. I made a phone call. I had a conversation. I spoke to the person I needed to speak to, and the words I needed came to me from somewhere. But to do all that I had to face my fears—of rejection, of confrontation, of naming the elephant in the room, and many more. When I did, I discovered that the other party to the conversation was also eager to move on. It could have gone differently. But however it had gone, I would still have moved on a little further in my place of passage.

✦

Take a little journey through the images we have explored. Do any of them speak to your situation? What specific fears do you see lurking in your heart regarding those situations?

Is there any practical way you can name them, face them, and go beyond them?

14

Yesterday Is Already Ours

A favorite mystery series of mine centers on a medieval Benedictine brother named Cadfael, an amateur sleuth. Cadfael walks the edges of orthodoxy and frequently falls foul of the monastic authorities. He also has a past. He was once in love with a beautiful woman, but their lives went down separate tracks. Then one day he meets her again, in older age. Both behave with perfect propriety, but it is obvious that the love still burns. The time comes for them to part again and pursue their separate vocations, and she asks, "Will we see each other again?" Cadfael ponders the question, then replies, thoughtfully: "In the certainty of heaven all we can be sure of is tomorrow. But since yesterday is already ours, what shall we fear?"

We may not feel as confident as Cadfael about "the certainty of heaven," but as people journeying in faith, we have committed ourselves, deep in our hearts, to trust that whatever the future holds, it will unfold in ways that ultimately, though perhaps not immediately or visibly, lead to more and more fullness of life, for each and for all. Through our journey in this book, we have seen in many different ways how good fruits grow from aspects of our circumstances that seem, at the time, frightening, threatening, and unwelcome. But what struck me most about Cadfael's comment was his affirmation that "yesterday is already ours."

One of our biggest fears, and the cause of so much resistance to change, is that we think we are on the verge of losing, irrevocably, what we value from our past. Yes, like Cadfael, we have a past. To be human is to have a past. Some of that past may be about things we wish we could put behind us forever and wipe clean from the slate of memory. Other things we cherish and dread losing. To embrace the unknown future that change and transition hold out to us is, we feel, to risk losing all that we have invested our lives in so far.

I think I learned something about letting go of the past when, many years ago, I had been through a period of fairly intensive spiritual growth. I was away from home at the time, actually attending a course my employer had sent me on—nothing remotely spiritual. My time away hadn't been a retreat in any conventional sense, but it had left me with the same kind of feeling that a retreat often grants us—that something very important had been given to me, much beyond anything I had learned on the course about how to do my job better. There had been frosty moonlit evenings and fresh early morning walks, during which prayer had seemed extraordinarily easy and had been very fruitful.

When it came time to leave, I didn't want to go. I remember telling God how much I wanted this graced time to continue. And then it felt as though these thoughts came across to me in prayer: "Walk on with empty hands, because I have so much more to give you in the future, and you can't receive it if your hands are full. Don't be afraid that in letting go you are losing anything at all, because everything that matters, from this time of graced encounter, or from any other experience in your life, has been internalized and is firmly lodged in your heart. It is yours. It is a part of you. It travels with you and can never be lost."

That was a real moment of truth for me. When you realize that all those experiences and encounters that lie in the past are not lost but have been absorbed into the heart of who you are, you find a new freedom to move forward. We internalize what matters. We can safely let go of what doesn't matter, just as our own bodies absorb all that is good and life-giving from what we feed them and let go of the waste. The old song that bemoans the fact that "every time we say good-bye, I die a little" expresses poignantly the fear of losing what has been so meaningful for us. But the truth is, as Cadfael says, that the past is already ours. Nothing can take from us the gift of all that our past has given us. We can't lose it, and it will play a crucial part in shaping our future. But this insight doesn't free us from the pangs of nostalgia when we are moving out of one phase of life and haven't quite arrived in the next, even though, as it is sometimes said, "nostalgia isn't what it used to be!"

For example, I notice that when I am in transition I cling to small tokens that remind me of the past: a favorite coffee mug that has survived the move or my child's first schoolbook, even though she now has children of her own. The big question for me is this: when I look at the cherished item that I am trying to carry through the shifting scenes of my life, am I trying to turn back the clock, or am I just wanting to remind myself that the past is still an active part of me? That coffee mug that you can't part with, for example, may become an excuse to wallow in regret for the job you left, the home you sold, or the country you once lived in. Or it might be a gentle reminder, every morning, that all those memories have become part of who you are now, and that you have every reason to revisit them with gratitude, but no reason to let them swallow you up in fantasies about how the grass was always greener in the field you left behind.

Wanting to turn back the clock and return to how things were is a very natural and human reaction to change, but there are two problems with it. First, the arrow of time, as we have already noticed, flies only forward. The past is a womb to which we cannot return, and the attitude of constantly wanting to return to it leads eventually to the mentality that underpins fundamentalism in all its forms—that desire to return to a simplistic certainty that experience has shown to be illusory.

Second, a desire to look back will never take us forward, but it can become a dead weight on our ability to move beyond ourselves toward the people God is dreaming us to be. If we really believe in resurrection, then, as we have seen, we sometimes have to let the patient die. The patient may be some cherished dream; a long-gone relationship; our health, wealth, youth, or beauty; or perhaps our way of practicing religion. We can choose to keep the patient on life support, always striving to maintain the status quo, but to do so may be to abort the paschal mystery in which new life arises out of what has been allowed to die.

I once had the privilege of visiting Ellis Island in New York's harbor, which was the reception center in times past for the many emigrants arriving in America from Europe. If ever there was a monument to transition, Ellis Island is it. There you can see some of the items these people brought with them from their past into their hoped-for future: photographs, Bibles and prayer books, and items that would prove that they had learned some craft or skill in their homeland, which might secure them employment in the new world they were entering. I think that the items underline the wisdom of Cadfael. The past is already ours; these photos and mementos remind us daily that this treasure that was ours is not lost but carried with us, not just in our bags but in our hearts. And the future is ours, too, to explore and, we hope, to make a contribution to. This isn't nostalgia. This is wisdom.

What treasure from your own past experiences or relationships do you feel has been internalized and forever absorbed into your heart? Notice how it continues to enrich you. It has been said that our memories are like a garden from which we can never be expelled. Which memories in your soul's garden are life-giving, making you feel more fully alive in the present moment and more hopeful for the future?

Is there anything that you cling to from the past that you feel may be holding you prisoner in false nostalgia and blocking your way ahead? The yearning to go back to what has passed can take over our consciousness to the extent that we actually fail to see, let alone respond to, the beckoning of the future and the joys and challenges of the present moment. Do you detect any symptoms like these in your present situation?

15

Will You Save Your Life or Spend It?

There's a commercial currently doing the rounds for, I think, an insurance provider, probably one of those organizations that projects retirement as a happy-ever-after phenomenon where partners who have barely seen each other for forty years learn overnight to do everything together in their newfound intimacy. The commercial states rather grandly that, now that you are retired, you can do whatever you wish with your time (given, of course, that you have invested in the advertiser and now have unlimited funds). What struck me in all this was the suggestion that we can choose to spend our time however we like, or, significantly, we can choose to give it away to others. What we can't do, of course, is save it, in the sense of hanging on to it, because time won't stand still long enough to be saved.

Life, being a continuum of time, can likewise be spent or given away to others or most likely some combination of the two. Because life, like time, doesn't stand still, we cannot save it, but this fact isn't so obvious. If we are honest, we discover that a lot of what we do is really about trying to save ourselves and our time. In particular, our religious language and doctrines focus a great deal on this saving, and our social systems also encourage us in various ways to save ourselves. You would think, when you see some of the ideals we let people set up for us, that the whole idea is to keep ourselves so well preserved that the ravages of time can't get at us, at least not until the final curtain. This reminds me of an incident when my father was asked his opinion about a bush in the neighbor's garden that had died suddenly and for no apparent reason. My father, a keen gardener, peered knowingly at the bush and pronounced that it seemed to be in perfect health, except for being dead. Is that our aim, when we finally arrive at the undertaker's door: to be in perfect health, except for the misfortune of our demise?

You can usually tell the difference between people who have tried, on the whole, to save their lives and those who have risked spending them. The savers are often quite comfortable financially and physically well preserved. They have, very sensibly, kept out of the sun and off the cigarettes, and they may look ten years younger than they really are. The spenders will have wrinkled faces and gnarled hands, and they may look ten years older than they really are. *No contest*, you might think. Who would choose to end up like a spender? But before you decide, just listen to their stories. My guess is that the savers' stories are of the Jane Austen variety, a bit constrained and polite, unfolding in a fairly circumscribed arena, and with "me" being a fairly major character on the cast. The spenders' stories are more like the Brontës. They could take you just about anywhere, and you'll be sitting on the edge of your seat as you go. "Me," though not written out of the plot completely, is just one character among many. The world at the end of the savers' stories is not much different from how it was at the beginning. At the end of the spender's stories, it could be a world transformed.

One such spender was a woman once featured on a television program about South Africa. She ran an orphanage for children of people who had died of HIV/ AIDS, and she threw herself into her task unstintingly, day and night. When asked what legacy she hoped her life would leave behind when she died, she answered:

"I hope that when I die I shall have spent, completely, every gift I have been given by God, and I hope to leave nothing behind except maybe a little footprint."

Life is a gift, and gifts are for spending.

All of this may sound obvious. Why, then, is there so much emphasis on the word *save* in our religious language? This thought led me to ponder the whole concept of Passover and what it means to us as we negotiate our life transitions. And it seems to me that there is a huge divide between what *Passover* means in the Old Testament and what it comes to mean in the New Testament.

Underpinning the Old Testament view of Passover is the story of how the people of Israel are to be saved from the visitation of the angel of death. In Exodus 12, we hear how Yahweh warns Moses to make due sacrifice to be saved from the devastation that Yahweh is about to wreak on the Egyptian oppressors. If they carry out the sacrifice properly, and according to complicated rules, and mark their door lintels with the blood of the sacrificed animal, then the angel of death will pass over them and leave them unharmed. They will be saved. However, this will be the prelude to their departure and their wanderings in the wilderness, on a journey of self-discovery and a trail to inner freedom to which we are all invited to participate.

Clearly, the Old Testament Passover is about being saved. But what about the New Testament Passover?

When Jesus celebrates Passover for the last time with his friends, there is no question of his being spared the visitation by the angel of death, nor is such a rescue offered to his friends or to us. In fact, he rebukes Peter robustly when Peter suggests that Jesus should not expose himself to the risk of crucifixion. Jesus will not be spared the worst that can happen. But in passing *through* it, he will transcend it. This takes the Passover journey to a very different level. Are we prepared to follow it beyond its Old Testament significance? Are we willing to acknowledge that our faith is not about being saved from harm but about transcending it by walking through it and in God's company?

The difference between Old Testament and New Testament Passover is something that perhaps we need to examine in our own attitudes and platitudes. Are we looking for a faith that protects us and keeps us safe? Do we think that if we carry out certain rituals according to complicated rules, we will be saved? It is too easy to settle for a simplistic understanding of faith as a rescue package. In subscribing to that outlook, we try to save our lives, when in fact we are invited to follow a man who, every moment and in every way, spends himself for others and for truth and justice, a man who invites us also to become life spenders. We are invited to become people on a quest not for rescue but for transformation. We are called beyond Exodus to Easter.

Before he faces his final days and the worst that life can throw at him in Jerusalem, Jesus makes an unscheduled journey to his friends Martha, Mary, and Lazarus in Bethany. While Jesus and his friends are still on the road, preaching and teaching, they receive the message that Lazarus is dangerously ill. What follows is very strange. Lazarus is a dear friend of Jesus, and yet Jesus, on hearing this news, delays before going to him in Bethany. Even given the time it would take for messages to cross the distance, his delay is a curious thing. Who knows what might have been going through Jesus' head at the time? He would have known, surely, that to act dramatically in Bethany would be to seal his own fate in Jerusalem, yet Jesus was never afraid to face the consequences of his actions. He hesitates, or so it appears. And then he tells his friends, cryptically, that "this illness does not lead to death" but to the greater glory of

God (John 11:4). After two days, and apparently already knowing that his friend is dead, Jesus makes the fateful decision: "Let us go to Judea again" (John 11:7). Both he and his friends knew that this would mean certain death for him, but he would not be deterred.

On arrival at Bethany, Jesus raises Lazarus from death, and he raises his own profile to a highly dangerous level. The incident triggers the sequence of events that leads him to the cross.

How might this story help us understand the movement from Old Testament Passover to New Testament Passover?

Jesus could have saved Lazarus if he had gone to him immediately, as Martha is quick to remind him (John 11:21). That would have been a kind of Old Testament rescue. Instead, he chose to delay, until Lazarus had died. In terms of our transition journey, we could say that he let Lazarus die. And then he goes on to reveal that his power is not about rescue but about transcendence. Lazarus, through the ministry of Jesus, transcends the power of death, but not before he has actually gone through it.

Whatever the facts may be surrounding this incident, the message is clear: "If you follow me, the angel of death will not pass over you and save you from what you fear, but you and I together will pass *through* the worst that you fear, and by doing so we will transcend it." To risk this journey, we will have to let some things die, as we have already seen, and not try to save them by clinging to them. That would be like saving the seeds of next year's crop and failing to plant them in the soil. There will be a crop next year only if we let the seeds rest in the winter soil and thereby liberate the new growth latent within them.

When Jesus calls Lazarus out of the grave, his first instruction to Lazarus's family and friends is "Unbind him" (John 11:44). He is, of course, asking them to release Lazarus from the restrictions of the shroud. Every time I read this phrase I am reminded of the German word *Entbindung*, which also means, literally, "unbinding," but its principal meaning is "giving birth." In English, we speak of a woman's confinement as she approaches the time to give birth. In German, the equivalent word is *Entbindung*. What a contrast! "Confinement" focuses on the restrictions on the mother-to-be and suggests a narrowing of focus. *Entbindung* focuses on the child who is coming to birth and suggests liberation and an opening up, or unbinding, of infinite possibilities. Jesus invites his friends to unbind Lazarus and thereby liberate him into a new level of life, thus transcending the power of death.

What is our response? Will we get stuck in an attitude of confinement, restricting our relationship with God to a rescue package that saves us (but may well leave others out in the cold)? Or dare we move forward, with Jesus, into the New Testament and allow ourselves to be unbound, given birth to, into and through the very things that we may well perceive as deaths?

A former colleague of mine was sent, as an eleven-year-old, to a summer camp run by a fairly extreme religious group. On his first night, he was surrounded by four very large teenage boys. He thought his end had come and they were going to assault him, until they demanded to know of him, "Have you been saved, lad?" He tells me he couldn't answer that question then, and he still can't, even though he is in ordained ministry.

My bet is that God isn't going to ask us, "Have you been saved?" but "Have you been spent? And if so, on what?"

Your life is a gift. Do you want, most of all, to save it?

Or are you willing, like Jesus, to spend it?

What is there in your own life that is genuinely

worth spending yourself for? How does this

look in practice?

Does the religious language of "being saved" help

or hinder you in your desire to spend yourself

for God and for others?

Does Christian faith and practice as you experience

them seem to focus more on an Old Testament or a

New Testament understanding of Passover?

16

Restoration? Renovation? Re-creation!

A kaleidoscope is a delightful instrument. An image created by a collection of small objects, such as beads or pebbles, is viewed through a series of reflecting mirrors. Turn the kaleidoscope even slightly, and the pattern will fall apart and re-create itself into a new shape. The kaleidoscope tells the story of this book in a simple shake. When the well-ordered and neatly arranged patterns in life fall apart, what happens next? We might be hoping for restoration, that somehow, by our own efforts or by the grace of God, or both, we will manage to get back to the old order that has broken down and so restore things to exactly how they were. Or we might realize that our lives needed a shake-up, but we still hope that this will be a breath of fresh air that will renew our efforts and our faith so that they more closely resemble what once fired our hearts until it takes on a new freshness. The kaleidoscope tells a different story. It reflects the experience we have of being shaken up, scattered into a thousand fragments, and coming back down again in a different order altogether. We can't make sense immediately of the new pattern. It takes us to a place we haven't been before: re-creation!

What does our faith journey mean in these terms? For many, faith is all about restoration. The idea is that we human beings were once without fault, until we went through a catastrophic "fall." In this scenario, the hope of faith is that we might be restored to our pristine innocence, that we might be saved from the consequences of our sinfulness. Faith thus becomes a nostalgic longing for what is perceived to have been eternally lost but that can be restored to us through the sacrificial death of an innocent victim. The faith of many Christians operates according to this premise.

For others, the journey of faith is rooted in the hope of renovation, or renewal—a determination to work with the Creator to help renew the face of the earth, especially in these times of such serious ecological crises. We speak of renewal missions, whose task is to reawaken the sometimes dormant fires of faith in a community of believers.

Renewal, of course, is always a good thing, but is it the whole story of what our faith is about?

Re-creation is something of an entirely different order. It involves risk. The eggshell must crack and the new life must emerge. The seed must lie in the ground, and the new growth must break through the cold earth. The dynamic of the Christian gospel is a dynamic of re-creation—of giving birth to something that is entirely new, yet truly reflects the shape and pattern of what has gone before. With every shake of the kaleidoscope, the pattern changes and remakes itself, and therein lies the delight.

There is a persistent urge in human beings to restore what has been broken, and if possible to put it back to exactly how it was. We restore old paintings and old books. There are even optimistic salespersons who would convince us that they can restore our lost youth. When Warsaw was destroyed in World War II, its citizens labored with tireless love to restore it to how it had been. And yet those who experience such works of restoration often report that they are left feeling somehow cheated, or at least unsatisfied. They long for something more.

The city of Dresden in the former East Germany is known mainly for the fact that it was firebombed in

February 1945 and largely obliterated. The Allied bombing raid that caused this destruction has since been widely condemned as a war crime, which cost thousands of innocent lives; Dresden, as was well known at the time, was not a military target, but it was full of refugees fleeing the Soviet advance from the east. One of the victims of that night's raid was the Frauenkirche, a Lutheran church of extraordinary beauty. Perhaps we might let the church tell its own story, for it is a story of restoration, which led to renewal, which became a re-creation:

> My story begins more than one hundred million years ago. Then I lay at the bottom of the sea and was being formed into solid rock by the continuous deposit of sand and decomposing organic material. My new life as solid sandstone was birthed in the dying of other material, and gradually I was shaped and formed, unseen, unguessed at, in the depths of the sea.
>
> Around eighty million years ago, the seas receded. The conflict continued, as my neighbors, a granite massif on one side and the so-called Ore Mountains on the other, pushed against me, reshaping me, sometimes forcefully, into the cuboid formations that came

to characterize me, and made me into a much-sought-after building material, especially for churches.

In the eleventh century, I became, for the first time, a church—a Romanesque church dedicated to Our Lady in the diocese of nearby Meissen. I stood my ground through the upheavals of the Reformation, when I became a Protestant church. A whole shift of thinking and believing was surging around me, just as once the seas had surged, and my spirit was being reshaped, though my body remained unchanged. In 1727, I was deemed too small, was pulled down, and was rebuilt as a fine Lutheran baroque church to provide space for more worshippers. My crowning glory was my dome, which soared to almost 320 feet above the city. It was known as the Stone Bell, and it became a distinctive landmark in the Dresden skyline.

But my life was never uneventful. I know both the terrible and the sublime. During the Seven Years' War, my dome was pummeled by the cannonballs of Frederick II and his armies, but they left me unharmed. And, unforgettably, on December 1, 1736, Johann Sebastian Bach gave a recital on my newly installed Silbermann organ. My dome swelled with pride.

And so my story continued, until February 13, 1945, when U.S. and British forces firebombed Dresden. For two days and two nights I stood firm. Refugees found sanctuary for a while in my crypt, and I held out against the hell of the bombardment just long enough to allow them to be evacuated, although there was nowhere to run to in that stricken city. Eventually, when the temperature inside me reached over 1800 degrees Fahrenheit, I collapsed, and six thousand tons of stone that the earth had once wrested from the seas plunged back to the earth and remained a pile of rubble for the next forty-five years.

But in 1982, a new and strange attractor began to move, as people longing for peace and freedom began to gather in my ruins. Over the following years, this tiny beginning swelled into a movement that was changing the face of Eastern Europe, culminating in 1989 in the fall of the infamous Berlin Wall and the collapse of the communist regimes across the countries of the region. In this new dispensation, there was talk of restoration—and of very generous gifting—and so, in 1994, the foundation stone was laid for my new incarnation. I was to be reconstructed exactly according to the plans of the old church, and using a large number of the stones that had been salvaged from my ruins.

The plan was to restore me, but over time it became clear that my rebirth was also becoming an exercise in renewal. I stood for the renewal of hope among the people of Dresden for a new era of freedom and faith. The very fact of my rebuilding renewed their energies and their passion. Big bene-factors and little people contributed their resources, including their time and labor, to my rebuilding. I remember most affectionately the little people, because their hearts burned with a desire not just for renovation but also for reconciliation. I remem-ber lovingly a group of Polish taxi drivers, who had themselves been victims of the Nazis during the war but wanted to bring their personal efforts into a labor of love, mutual understanding, and a new beginning for all the people. And I remember how the gilded orb and cross that now crowns my dome was made by a London silversmith, Alan Smith, whose father had been part of the aircrew that had destroyed me in 1945, and who, his son recalled, had always believed that the bombardment had been an immoral act.

On the day of my rededication, I knew for sure that, although in outward appearance I was almost identical to my fallen ancestor, my inner spirit was something entirely new. The bishop who consecrated me spoke of how a seed has to fall into the ground and die before the new thing can be born from it, and I knew in every stone that the spirit that had reshaped me was such a seed. From a candle lit in my ruins, so fragile, so easily blown out, the surge of longing for the new beginning had grown and grown until I had risen from the ashes to become a statement of all human desire and determination that peace should forever displace enmity.

Mine is a hundred-million-year story of many destructions and many restorations, of much breakdown and subsequent renewal, but above all, it is a story of how God, true to God's promise, is constantly making all things new.

✦

As you look back over the story of your own life,

or the life of your family, community, or nation,

where do you see the desire for renewal and

re-creation manifesting itself? How can you

cooperate in your own way, using your own gifts,

with this re-creating spirit?

Do you think it is possible to get stuck in trying to

reconstruct things to how they were and lose sight

of the challenge to let them become the new thing

that God is constantly longing to bring to birth?

Where do you see this danger revealing itself in

the world or the church today? How might we

discover for ourselves, and share with others, a

renewed trust in the God who is constantly making

all things new and does so most frequently through

our experience of breakdown?

17

Adapt, Survive, Transcend

Throughout the course of evolution, survival has depended on adaptation. The creatures most able to adapt to sometimes dramatically changed conditions were the ones that survived. When we made the voyage with Noah earlier in this journey, we were actually observing adaptation in action. Noah and his family were the ones who adapted to the changed situation. The rest drowned.

What does this natural phenomenon say to us in our complex transitions in today's world, where it is no longer a matter of growing warmer fur or longer legs but the kind of transition that demands engagement at all levels: physical, intellectual, and spiritual? And is it always a good idea to adapt? What if we are adapting to situations that we really should be resisting? Nothing is black and white anymore.

The pattern we observe in the natural world suggests that adaptation makes it possible to survive in changed conditions but that survival is not always in the form we recognized before. Species really do become extinct and give way on our planet to new arrivals. We know that this is the case in the created world, but we prefer not to look at the possibility that it might also apply to our own species, *Homo sapiens*. Surely, we think, we are the pinnacle of creation, that God's creativity has arrived in us; we are its peak manifestation on planet Earth, and we are here to stay.

That might be a foolish and an arrogant dream. Whether by our own mindless exploitation of the planet's resources or by some natural disaster, pandemic, or combination of these, our future—in our present state—is by no means assured on this earth. We don't want to contemplate this possibility. We cling very much, in this context, to the ideal of saving ourselves, of preserving the species intact, and of continuing to enjoy the life we lead at the top of the food chain. (It's interesting that there are only two serious predators to humankind, if you don't go putting yourself in the way of lions and tigers. One is tiny: the virus. The other is man sized: it is ourselves.)

Because we have come so far in our explorations of the crazy universe of change and faced many of the hazards along the way, let's go one step further and just imagine the unimaginable: *Homo sapiens* becomes extinct. In the face of such a threat, do the words *adapt, survive, transcend* have any meaning at all?

We may find it hard to imagine what God could possibly do to better us! But the possibility of extinction, or near extinction, may well give rise to a situation in which only a remnant of humanity survives, and that remnant will have to make very big adjustments to a new way of being on the planet. And transcendence? Well, many spiritual thinkers and dreamers, in many different ways, have suggested that the human family may be engaged in a spiritual evolution of which we are barely aware. There is some evidence that, in the rising tide of searching for spiritual expression and meaning in our lives, a heightening of spiritual consciousness is indeed in process and that we are involved in it, whether or not we are aware of our involvement.

In the evolution section of the Paris Science Museum there is a notice reading: "the process of hominization [meaning the physical evolution of humankind] may still not be complete, but the process of *humanization* has barely begun." Spiritual evolution would be about this process of humanization—about becoming fully human, the people God is dreaming us to be—and it is already expressing itself in the ways we choose to be in the world:

- In the generosity of spirit with which so many people respond when other people, or indeed other creatures, suffer disaster
- In the growing realization that this earth is a living organism, of which we are an interdependent part and that we have no right to exploit
- In the increasing understanding that unbridled consumerism is not making us more human but is actually tending to dehumanize us, especially when it happens at the expense of our brothers and sisters in lands where poverty is the norm
- In the growing distrust of, and opposition to, military solutions to solve disputes and the demand for more mature solutions to be sought to resolve conflict
- In the escalating search for spiritual meaning in our lives, often expressing itself beyond the boundaries of organized religion

- ◄ In the realization that our right-brain capabilities of intuition and creativity need to balance our overdeveloped left-brain skills of logic and organization
- ◄ In the growing distrust of hierarchy in favor of consensus and co-accountability.
- ◄ In the growing understanding that our future will depend on cooperation rather than on competition

Of course there are plenty of contraindications. The darkness will always fight back hard when light begins to dawn. But if these signs of change are genuine and lasting, they could truly be the beginnings of transcendence. We may actually already be beginning to transcend the self-focused and adversarial attitudes that define many of our interpersonal and international relationships at present, and be moving into new ways of being human. We may actually be becoming something beyond *Homo sapiens*, something closer to God's dream, something incarnated and modeled in the life and death of Jesus of Nazareth, who alone among us has transcended the boundary of death that seems to us so absolute.

The good news is that we have the choice to cooperate with this process of transcendence, nurturing all that is making us more human and working against all that is tending to dehumanize us. Then, perhaps it will become more important to us to spend our lives and our energy in ways that further this dream than to rigidly save them in the hope of clinging to the way of being we know as *Homo sapiens*. Once the chick has hatched, the parents will no longer grieve over the broken shell. Can it be so for us, too?

Meanwhile, we find ourselves in the midst of transition, and this might be a good point at which to reflect on a few practical ideas to help us navigate these rapids. The suggestions that follow are not in any particular order of importance. Use any that seem helpful to you, and leave aside those that are not. Feel free to add your own survival tips.

Live primarily in the new mind-set, defined by your new situation, not the old one.

Let the new mind-set be your baseline. Seasoned travelers recommend that when you land in a new time zone, the best way to overcome jet lag is to move immediately into that new time zone; so, for example, if you have turned your watch back, then you should try to stay awake until everyone else is ready to go to bed. In the same way, we can set our minds to the new situation, whatever it might be, rather than constantly harking back to "how things were."

Approach the transition by viewing it primarily as a birth, not a death.

Something has been lost, but something new is beginning. Try to experience the losses involved in transition not so much as death rehearsals, but, more creatively, as prenatal classes.

Maintain a creatively critical stance toward the transition.

What aspects are making you feel more alive, more fully human? Cooperate with those aspects. Is anything in this transition tending to make you feel less alive, less fully human, or tending to dehumanize all of us? Work against those aspects. There isn't an option to stay neutral. Not all transitions are good news. We don't have to engage with every change that our culture or society tries to thrust on us.

Give yourself time to catch up with the speed
of change.

Give yourself time, or if necessary, take whatever steps you can to slow down the speed of change. Be gentle with yourself. Give yourself downtime to adjust to new situations.

Reflect on the legacy of anything you feel you have
lost or had to leave behind.

The past has gifts for you. Receive them with an open heart and use them as you move forward. Even, perhaps especially, your perceived failures from the past may be a source of great growth in the future. What remnants of the past will you use as compost for future growth?

Don't try to adapt to structures that are
themselves distorted.

Much pain in our lives comes from forcing ourselves to adapt to things that are themselves inherently wrong. Many people feel a false guilt, for example, when they experience discomfort or tension in trying to conform to the structures of a particular religious system or social organization. Ask yourself, "Should I be trying to adapt to these structures, which I question, or should I be trying to change the structures, so that they come more into line with what my own integrity, or the integrity of the human family as a whole, requires?

Shed baggage.

Pioneers move only if they travel light. Remember that what matters has already become absorbed and integrated into the core of your being, and you cannot lose it. Risk walking on with empty hands, ready to receive with gratitude all the new gifts and insights God is longing to give you.

Accept responsibility for what happens to your life.

We have choices, even in situations that appear to be forced on us. One freedom can never be taken from us: the freedom to choose our attitude in every situation. Take ownership of the transitions in your life. We don't have to accept a state of complete helplessness in the face of transition. Be aware of the danger of presenting ourselves as helpless so that others will resolve our problems. This can become a self-fulfilling prophecy, seducing us into a passive response to change when we sometimes need to be proactive.

Allow yourself to grieve for your losses.

Acknowledge the very real pain involved in your "deaths." Grief is a process that takes time, and sometimes a long time. When you have had to let go of a lifestyle, a beloved home, a career, or a cherished dream, such a loss is a very real bereavement and must be respected as such.

Face your fears.

Don't live in denial of them. Let God take you to the encounter with fear itself, not just the immediate causes of that fear. Notice the shape and form of your particular fears. This might be an invitation to grow inwardly as, with God, you gently move beyond them.

Remember other times of transition that you have already navigated.

What can you learn from them? What helpful patterns do they show you about how to come through change? Do they show you anything that you would not want to repeat in your new process of transition? Don't make any judgments. Simply learn from your story.

Focus on the deepest center, the core of your being.

Where is the solid ground in your life? What matters most to you? Which parts of your life feel as though they are built on sand and which are built on rock?

Envision the future as you would like it to become.

Dream big! We are the cocreators, with God, of our own future. What do you want that future to look like, and how can you work toward making that future a reality?

Seek and nourish community.

We are not asked to face change and transition alone. We are made for community. We are asked to be midwives, or facilitators to one another. How can you make this happen in practical ways? Where and/or who is your community? Who are your midwives? Can you help facilitate another's birthing?

Apply the wisdom of twelve-step spirituality.

Seek the courage to change what must be changed, the patience to accept what cannot be changed, and the wisdom to know the difference.

✦

How do you feel about the possibility that a spiritual

evolution is happening and that your everyday

choices are helping shape the direction of

that evolution?

What practical wisdom would you offer from your

own experience to help others deal with the

changes and transitions they face?

18

It's a Bit Muddy . . .

A friend sent me a card with a picture of Moses leading the children of Israel through the Red Sea. The waters had parted, and the people were tramping across the sea-bed while towering waves rose up on either side. The caption on the card, purporting to be Moses's comment to his complaining followers read, "What do you mean, 'It's a bit muddy!'?"

Here we are, on a journey that is leading us, we believe, ever closer to a mystery that longs to transform us and our world and all creation into everything we are capable of becoming, and what do we do? We complain about the state of our footwear. The picture is so very human that it is really quite consoling. We are, at least, all in the mud together, and neither Moses nor God is about to give up on us.

We noticed that, although the Old Testament Passover was about getting saved, it was the prelude to a journey, and that journey requires us to go through the mud and not be rescued from it. We are still making this journey today, and if we let the spirit of Exodus guide us, it can shed ancient light and wisdom on the very contemporary challenges we face in our current transitions.

So I invite you to make this journey now, in the context of your own situations and the situations we face in our world. You might like to pause at each part of the journey to reflect on what it has to say to your own experience of dislocation and transition, and what, if anything, it has to say to the global situations that affect all of us.

The Chaos from Which New Possibility Arises

The story of Passover begins from a place of exploitation, cruelty, and violence (Exodus 1–2). Moses has been provoked to an act of revenge and desperation, and he is feeling the pangs of guilt that follow. He takes flight after killing the Egyptian oppressor.

How would you describe your own chaos? And the world's chaos? What are your own feelings?

A Leader Is Called Forth

Moses's situation is a classic story of God calling the least likely candidate. Moses is implicated in the uprising, hardly a hero but neither a yes-man. He has the normal human mixture of rage, remorse, fear, and disorientation. God calls him out of the midst of his worst moment (Exodus 3). But Moses isn't going to come quietly. He certainly doesn't suffer from any Messiah complex. He pleads that he can't do the task at hand and comes up with all kinds of excuses: he isn't good with words (so God sends him Aaron, who is); he doesn't even know who it is who is calling him (so God gives him an answer in Exodus 3:14: "I am who I am"). Finally he pleads that no one will take him seriously, and God says, "Do it anyway" (Exodus 6–7).

But note God's side of the contract. What God gives to Moses is a vision (the burning bush), a profound experience of the Holy One, and an empowerment far beyond Moses's own resources.

Do you have any sense of God calling you to move beyond whatever impasse you are facing? How does that feel? How does the call reveal itself? What personal vision might empower you to go beyond crisis to opportunity?

What about God's call to all of us to move beyond where we are and to transcend the fears that paralyze us in our global situation? Where will we find leadership? To what extent are we asked to provide leadership or to cooperate with the leadership we believe to be motivated by integrity? As a backdrop to this calling, listen to Moses's complaints that "God isn't doing anything" (Exodus 6). Have you ever said things like that? And hear God's answer: "I am doing something— I'm calling you!"

The First Wave of Resistance

Once the call has been accepted and the journey of transition embraced, things get really tough. When we live true to God's dream of who we can become, we provoke the dark side of our humanity to rise up to engulf us. In the Old Testament Passover story, the dark side takes the form of rivers that turn to blood—we can see them flowing even now, in Afghanistan, in Palestine, in Africa. The dark side takes the form of the plagues that afflict the oppressors, but not just the oppressors; everyone is affected, which culminates in the death of every firstborn son.

> We still see the soldiers coming home in body bags, the sons and the daughters, the lovers and the friends, and we know that just as many innocent civilians have also lost their lives. Violence begets violence, yesterday, today and—does it have to go on into tomorrow (Exodus 7)? How might we resist these manifestations of the dark side of humanity? Can we challenge violence without becoming violent ourselves?

Leaving the Comfort Zone

Egypt can perhaps hardly be called a comfort zone, and yet the children of Israel are strangely reluctant to leave it. They are instructed to celebrate Passover quickly, and to leave in haste, carrying almost nothing with them. They are driven out. They are dislocated. They are expelled. But what is in human terms an expulsion is, in God's hands, a birthing. They don't even have time for a meal, but have to be content with unleavened bread that they can carry with them and that won't spoil so easily (Exodus 12).

✦

What does "Egypt" mean for you? What does it mean for our world today? What is the old order that has let us down and driven us out into the wilderness?

How are you entering the transition journey? What are you carrying with you? Are you trying to take the old order along with you even as you leave it all behind? Do you want to have your cake and eat it, too? Pilgrims always travel light; if they don't, they won't make the distance. What, for you, is the hardest thing to leave behind? What will you miss most? Naming it can be the first step to letting it go.

And we come to the crux of Old Testament Passover spirituality: if you keep the law, the angel of death will pass over you and not harm you. Jesus overturns this, as he overturns all our old assumptions, by revealing that the worst thing you fear may actually happen to you, but it cannot ultimately destroy you, not in the core of your being. Ultimately, if you trust the process, you will transcend it and come through to something you had never imagined. Jesus doesn't just say this, but he lives it, dies it, lets it apparently destroy him, and then transcends it. This is a vital difference between the spirituality of Passover in the Old and New Testaments.

> ✦
>
> What about you? Are you still expecting Old Testament protection, or will you risk New Testament transcendence?
> And so the children of Israel leave Egypt after 430 years of slavery and oppression. How long have you been in your personal Egypt? Dare you leave it and set your face toward the new dawn, even if doing so takes you into the wilderness?

The spirituality of Passover will always ask us to remember the story of where we were, how we left, and how we and God together made the journey through the consequences (Exodus 13). This story is retold in every Jewish family at every Passover meal to this day and in every Christian celebration of Eucharist.

> What helps you remember your personal story and
> celebrate the action of God in your life so far?

The Wilderness Experience

The pilgrims in the Exodus story are guided by a pillar of cloud by day and a pillar of fire by night, as they make their way through the wilderness (Exodus 13).

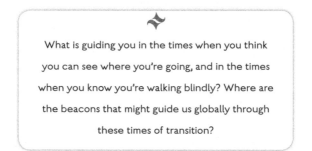

> What is guiding you in the times when you think
> you can see where you're going, and in the times
> when you know you're walking blindly? Where are
> the beacons that might guide us globally through
> these times of transition?

The pilgrims are taken by God on a roundabout route, not the direct and obvious way, because God doesn't intend for them to ever find their way back (Exodus 13).

✦

How do you feel about the decree, "There is no way back"? We have embarked on a journey that has only one direction: forward. Things will never be the same again. Take time to let that truth come to rest and take root in your heart and mind. Feel the pain of it, and then, in God's grace and in your own time, move on.

They carry the body of Joseph with them (Exodus 13). Joseph is the dreamer. Symbolically they carry their dreams through the desert.

✦

What dreams do you need to carry with you as you negotiate the wilderness of your transitional experience? What dreams does the world need to carry now as we enter a very different world order from anything we've known before?

Crossing the Red Sea

In any transition there comes a decisive moment when we cross a line, and we know that we are stepping right into the unknown. Like Indiana Jones, we are stepping into an abyss, and we will find out whether or not there is a bridge only after we have stepped out with one foot into the void.

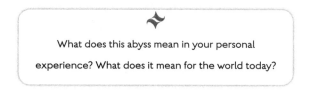

What does this abyss mean in your personal experience? What does it mean for the world today?

The cloud that makes things dark and impenetrable for the Egyptians actually gives light to those who are risking the transit (Exodus 14).

Thinking about the Exodus story, what parts of your own experience do you feel are part of "Egypt" and therefore in the dark, and what parts are "Israel" and therefore being guided, however faintly, toward a new beginning? What about the whole human family? How willing are we to take the risk? Do we have a choice?

When the Egyptians try to pursue their quarry, the waves that parted for the pilgrims return to engulf their enemies. We are a bit too quick to suggest that God is always "on our side" in any conflict, including in our twenty-first-century military confrontations. We still, perhaps, cherish the hope that God will simply eliminate our enemies and all will be well. But Jesus challenges us to love our enemies—that is, to act toward them in the most loving, life-giving way we can, however we might feel. Yet the power of this story is not diminished for all this: there are much subtler "enemies" trying to ensnare us than the armies of the "other side." As we make our journey through the wilderness, we are pursued by the forces of uninhibited consumerism, selfish acquisitiveness, careless lifestyles that put others' very existence in jeopardy, apathy in the face of injustice, collusion with agents of violence and oppression, and the list goes on.

> Which "enemies" do you feel are pursuing you? Do
> you trust that God can take you beyond them, show
> you how to transcend them?

Sustained in the Desert
But God does not leave Moses and the people to perish in the wilderness, and God will not abandon us there

either, if we really trust in this process of transition. As they journey, they find unexpected sources of life, for example:

Bitter waters are made potable (Exodus 15).

Twelve springs and seventy palm trees are discovered (Exodus 15).

There is food in the form of manna and quails (Exodus 16).

There is fresh water springing from the hardest rock (Exodus 17).

✦

What sustains you in your own desert?

What do you think the world needs now to sustain

us through these desert times?

What part might God be asking you to play in

supplying what the world community needs?

A Very Human Response

Not gratitude, but grumbling! Although we can imagine that forty years of eating manna and quails might not be everyone's idea of a good time, we can identify with the reaction of the petulant pilgrims and their sorely tried leader.

There are complaints; there is conflict (Exodus 17).

There are regrets that they ever set out; in Egypt, at least they had their leeks and cauliflowers and cucumbers. They have selective memories when it comes to other matters such as slavery. This scene was reenacted dramatically when the Berlin Wall fell. Within weeks there were people saying openly that they wanted the wall back. Under communism they had known where they were and had not had to take personal responsibility for their lives. They remembered cheap food and fuel and guaranteed employment. They forgot that they hadn't been able to speak freely with their neighbors, to travel, or to have a vote on how they were governed.

> Have you ever felt regret yourself that you left the relative comfort of unfreedom to follow your dream into the unknown?
> Where do we see this kind of grumbling going on today in our world and in ourselves?

There is a great emphasis on law. The people of Israel begin to choke on their own legislation, as more and more detailed regulations emerge. So do we! This tendency is very apparent in some of our own societies and institutions. Our "wilderness" bristles with cameras and small-print regulations very reminiscent of the Exodus world. In religious practice, we are tempted to think that if we make the rules difficult enough, we will be saved.

Jesus will override all of this and show us that the way to transcendence is not primarily through the law but through love; not through our own efforts but by grace alone.

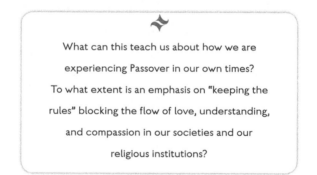

What can this teach us about how we are experiencing Passover in our own times? To what extent is an emphasis on "keeping the rules" blocking the flow of love, understanding, and compassion in our societies and our religious institutions?

There is heavy emphasis in the later chapters of Exodus on religious practice. This is Old Testament spirituality. New Testament spirituality rates compassion higher than observance. The spiritual journey is about nourishing a living fire, not about worshipping the ashes.

Does our own religious practice ever rate observance higher than compassion? Are the demands of orthodoxy stifling our spiritual imagination? Is there anything we need to challenge in the systems that define our religious practices?

There is a constant temptation to settle for less. God appears conspicuous by God's apparent absence in the desert, and so the people make themselves a lesser god that they can see, and we have the memorable image of the golden calf, a man-made image that they substitute for the spirit of a living God (Exodus 32).

What shape does the golden calf take for us now? Do you see any "golden calves" around? You might notice it, for example, in shopping malls, in celebrity cults, on sports fields, and even (perhaps especially) in some of our own cherished religious practices.

But the place of divine encounter is a tent—representing a place where human beings encounter the power of God and known by them as the tent of meeting. God is understood by Moses and his people to be a power on the move. Although they don't know it, the children of Israel are already making the journey toward the breakthrough of the New Testament. The cloud of God's presence hovers over the tent and never leaves it (Exodus 40). God accompanies us right in the very heart of our processes of transition and never leaves us.

What does this mean for our New Testament journey, our personal journey, our global journey? Could it be that the crisis in which we find ourselves is not primarily personal or economic or geophysical, but spiritual?
Where will we discover the more mature spiritual vision that might guide us closer to Everything God dreams we can become? Take time to reflect on these observations and to dwell especially on any aspect of the Exodus journey that speaks to you particularly. What is God saying to you personally through this ancient story? What is God saying to all of us collectively?

Our journeys through change and transition may challenge us to the core, burning away the dross in our lives and revealing the nugget of gold right at the heart of our being, where God is waiting to disclose Godself in ourselves and our world. Let's not allow a bit of mud to put us off!

.

19

Some Transitions in Scripture

Scripture is full of stories of change and transition—an open invitation to soak ourselves in their ancient wisdom and learn from them some guidance on how to navigate the rapids of our own lives.

You might like to use some of those stories as you continue the journey through your life's transitions and upheavals, perhaps reading them through slowly and noticing any words or images that especially speak to your heart, and then recognizing any connections with your own situation that God is offering for your consideration.

- Genesis 9: The story of Noah.
- Genesis 12:1: The call of Abraham to "go from your country and your kindred and your father's house to the land that I will show you."

- ⤙ Genesis 28:10–22: Jacob's dream of the ladder connecting heaven and earth, and his realization, "The Lord is in this place—and I did not know it!" (Genesis 28:16)
- ⤙ Exodus 1–18: the full story of the journey of the children of Israel from slavery to freedom.
- ⤙ Deuteronomy 1:6–7: "You have stayed long enough at this mountain. Resume your journey."
- ⤙ Ruth 1:16: "Where you go, I will go."
- ⤙ Psalm 46: God's presence in the midst of turmoil.
- ⤙ Psalm 91:5: "You will not fear the terror of the night . . ."
- ⤙ Psalm 126:5: "May those who sow in tears reap with shouts of joy."
- ⤙ Ecclesiastes 3:1–8: "There is a season for everything."
- ⤙ Isaiah 42:16: "I will lead the blind by a road they do not know, by paths they have not known I will guide them."
- ⤙ Isaiah 43:1–7: "Do not fear, for I have redeemed you."
- ⤙ Isaiah 48:6: "From this time forward I make you hear new things, hidden things that you have not known."

- Isaiah 54:10: "For the mountains may depart and the hills be removed, but my steadfast love shall not depart from you."
- Isaiah 65:17–20: "I am about to create new heavens and a new earth."
- Jeremiah 29:11–14: "I know what plans I have for you . . . plans for your welfare and not for harm."
- Baruch 2:30–35: "But in the land of their exile they will come to themselves."
- Ezekiel 37:1–14: The dry bones are brought to life.
- Hosea 2:14: "I am going to seduce her and lead her into the desert and speak to her heart."
- Joel 2:25: "I will repay you for the years that the swarming locust has eaten."
- Joel 2:28: "I shall pour out my spirit on all humanity. Your sons and daughters shall prophesy, your old people shall dream dreams, and your young people see visions."
- Book of Jonah: A story of resistance, and then surrender, to the movements of grace through the darkness of disaster.
- Matthew 7:24–27: The house built on rock and the house built on sand.
- Matthew 9:16–17: New wine in old wineskins.

- ◄ Matthew 13:31–32: The parable of the mustard seed; great things grow from tiny seeds.
- ◄ Mark 10:17–22: A rich young man pulls back from the brink of transformation.
- ◄ Luke 5:4: "Put out into the deep water and let down your nets for a catch."
- ◄ Luke 14:28–35: Counting the cost of transformation.
- ◄ Luke 15:11–32: The prodigal son makes his own journey through the wilderness.
- ◄ Luke 19:1–10: Zacchaeus experiences a wholly unexpected transition.
- ◄ Luke 24:13–35: A transformative encounter occurs on the road to Emmaus.
- ◄ John 1:39: "Come and see."
- ◄ John 4:1–42: Jesus' encounter with the woman at the well, a transformative encounter for them both and for her entire village.
- ◄ John 11:1–44: Lazarus is raised from the dead.
- ◄ John 20:17: "Do not hold on to me."
- ◄ Romans 8:22: "The whole creation has been groaning in labour pains until now."
- ◄ Revelation 21:5–7. "I am the Alpha and the Omega, the beginning and the end."

20

As You Move On . . .

Jesus commissions his friends to venture forth into an unknown future, where he well knows they will meet many difficulties, challenges, and dangers. This is what he tells them (in Mark 6:8):

- ⤙ Take nothing for the journey, except a staff— no bread, no bag, no money in your belts.
- ⤙ Wear sandals and don't take a spare tunic.
- ⤙ Where people welcome you and the message you bring, stay in that place.
- ⤙ Where you are not welcomed, shake the dust off from under your feet and move on.

The exodus from Egypt must have looked very much like this. The children of Israel, as they embarked on their journey from unfreedom to freedom, also had to move quickly, to set off with just their sandals and staffs, carrying only their dreams and unleavened bread, and trusting the wilderness to sustain them.

Our journeys have much in common with theirs. We don't know where the future is taking us or what we will encounter along the way. We know we are leaving a lot behind, and yet that which matters most is always with us. We may be glad to be leaving some things behind, and for other things we will grieve bitterly. Yet in our hearts we know there is no way back. If we try to carry our baggage with us, we will get stuck at the first hurdle, unable to carry the weight of all that we think we can't live without. So, for us, too, there will be no bread, no emergency pack of things we have squirreled away for a rainy day. And yet we can, and we should, carry a lump of sourdough with us, because whatever has shaped our past will become the new beginning of our future. No fragment of our experience, however painful it may have felt, is lost or wasted, in the growing of God's dream.

There will be no money, because the currency we need for this journey is the currency of the heart and is counted in courage, not cash.

There will be no backpack, because what we need is already embedded in our hearts, and the less we try to save, the more freely we will be able to spend ourselves and our lives.

But, we will have sandals, and we will have a staff.

Have you ever wondered, "Why the staff?"

An old riddle used to pose the question: "What first has four legs, then two, and finally three?"

The answer of course is: the human person, who crawls on all fours as a baby, and then walks upright as a grown person, and finally needs a cane for support in old age.

The journey through change to transformation is a journey for the mature soul. And the mature soul knows that there is no way of making this journey under his or her own steam. The staff is there to remind us that we need something—Someone—to lean on.

The dependency of childhood has gone, and the independence we so cherish in our adult life may be taken from us at any moment by chance or circumstance. When that happens, we are pitched into the chaotic world of change and growth.

As you go, you will meet with situations that take you closer to the God who dreams within you and to the heart of what it means to be human. Stay with those situations and lend them your energy.

And you will meet with situations that mock your dream, despise your heart's truth, and work against the coming of God's dream. Shake them off like mud from your shoes, and leave them behind.

Walk in your own, and not in another's, sandals, for your journey is yours alone. No one else can make it for you, nor can you walk with integrity in the path destined for another.

Walk on, in courage and in hope, leaning on the only staff you know you can trust, and one day, when you least expect it, you will wake to find yourself on the other side of chaos.